ON ELIZABETH BISHOP

WRITERS ON WRITERS

COLM TÓIBÍN ▨ ON ELIZABETH BISHOP

PRINCETON UNIVERSITY PRESS

Princeton and Oxford

Requests for permission to reproduce material from this work should be sent to Permissions, Princeton University Press

Owing to limitations of space, all acknowledgments for permission to reprint previously published material can be found on page 207.

Published by Princeton University Press, 41 William Street, Princeton, New Jersey 08540
In the United Kingdom: Princeton University Press, 6 Oxford Street, Woodstock, Oxfordshire OX20 1TW

press.princeton.edu

Jacket photograph © Bettman/CORBIS. Courtesy of Vassar College Archives and Special Collections.

Cover photograph courtesy of Vassar College Archives and Special Collections.

ISBN 978-0-691-15411-4

Library of Congress Control Number: 2014951285

British Library Cataloging-in-Publication Data is available

This book has been composed in Minion Pro and Myriad Pro
Printed on acid-free paper. ∞
Printed in the United States of America

10 9 8 7 6 5 4 3 2 1

For Hedi El Kholti

▨ CONTENTS

■ ON ELIZABETH BISHOP

No Detail Too Small

She began with the idea that little is known and that much is puzzling. The effort, then, to make a true statement in poetry—to claim that something *is* something, or *does* something—required a hushed, solitary concentration. A true statement for her carried with it, buried in its rhythm, considerable degrees of irony because it was oddly futile; it was either too simple or too loaded to mean a great deal. It did not do anything much, other than distract or briefly please the reader. Nonetheless, it was essential for Elizabeth Bishop that the words in a statement be precise and exact. "Since we do float on an unknown sea," she wrote to Robert Lowell, "I think we should examine the other floating things that come our way carefully; who knows what might depend on it?" In her poem "The Sandpiper," the bird, a version of the poet herself, was "a student of Blake," who celebrated seeing "a World in a Grain of Sand / And a Heaven in a Wild Flower."

A word was a tentative form of control. Grammar was an enactment of how things stood. But nothing was stable, so words and their structures could lift and have resonance, could move out, take in essences as a sponge soaks in water.

Thus language became gesture in spite of itself; it was rooted in simple description, and then it bloomed or withered; it was suggestive, had a funny shape, or some flourishes, or a tone and texture that had odd delights, but it had all sorts of limits and failures. If words were a cry for help, the calm space around them offered a resigned helplessness.

In certain societies, including rural Nova Scotia where Bishop spent much of her childhood, and in the southeast of Ireland where I am from, language was also a way to restrain experience, take it down to a level where it might stay. Language was neither ornament nor exaltation; it was firm and austere in its purpose. Our time on the earth did not give us cause or need to say anything more than was necessary; language was thus a form of calm, modest knowledge or maybe even evasion. The poetry and the novels and stories written in the light of this knowledge or this evasion, or in their shadow, had to be led by clarity, by precise description, by briskness of feeling, by no open displays of anything, least of all easy feeling; the tone implied an acceptance of what was known. The music or the power was in what was often left out. The smallest word, or the holding of breath, could have a fierce, stony power.

Writing, for Bishop, was not self-expression, but there was a self somewhere, and it was insistent in its presence yet tactful and watchful. Bishop's writing bore the marks, many of them deliberate, of much re-writing, of things that had been said, but had now been erased, or moved into the shadows. Things measured and found too simple and obvious, or too loose in their emotional contours, or too philosophical, were removed. Words not true enough were cut away. What remained was then of value, but mildly so; it was as much as could be said, given the constraints. This great modesty was also, in its way, a restrained but serious ambition. Bishop merely seemed to keep her sights low; in her fastidious version of things, she had a sly system for making sure that nothing was beyond her range.

Bishop was never sure. In the last line of her poem "The Unbeliever," she has her protagonist state that the sea "wants to destroy us all," but the last line of "Filling Station" will read: "Somebody loves us all." In the poetics of her uncertainty surrounding the strange business of "us all," there was something hurt and solitary. In the first poem in her first book, a poem called "The Map," it was as though the world itself had to be studied as a recent invention or something that would soon fade and might need to be remembered as precisely as possible by a single eye.

For her, the most difficult thing to do was to make a statement; around these statements in her poems she created a hard-won aura, a strange sad acceptance that this statement was all that could be said. Or maybe there was something more, but it had escaped her. This space between what there was and what could be made certain or held fast often made her tone playful, in the same way as a feather applied gently to the inner nostril makes you sneeze in a way that is amused as much as pained.

In an early essay on Gerard Manley Hopkins, Bishop wrote about "motion" in poetry: "the releasing, checking, timing, and repeating of the movement of the mind according to ordered systems." Hopkins, she wrote, "has chosen to stop his poems, set them to paper, at the point in their development where they are still incomplete, still close to the first kernel of truth or apprehension which gave rise to them." Thus the idea of statement in Hopkins, the bare sense of a fact set down, offers a revelation oddly immediate and sharp, true because the illusion needs to be created that nothing else was true at the time the poem was written. And that making a statement has the same tonal effect as recovering from a shock, recovering merely for the time necessary to say one thing, including something casual and odd, and to leave much else unsaid.

Thus a line in a poem is all that can be stated; it is surrounded by silence as sculpture is by space. Hopkins could begin a poem: "I wake and feel the fell of dark not day." Or "No worst, there is none." Or "Summer ends now." Only then, once the bare statement had been made—something between a casual diary entry and something chiseled into truth—could the poem begin to be released and then controlled "according to ordered systems."

Bishop would begin poems with lines such as "I caught a tremendous fish" or "Here is a coast; here is a harbor" or "September rain falls on the house" or "Still dark" or "The sun is blazing and the sky is blue," and manage even in such inauspicious openings a tone that attended to the truth of things, a tone also of mild, distracted, solitary unease in the face of such truth.

In her poems Bishop often corrected herself, or qualified herself, almost as a duty or a ceremony. In the second line of "The Map" she wrote the word "Shadows," and then immediately wondered "or are they shallows"; in "The

Weed," she wrote, in a dream, "I lay upon a grave, or bed" but immediately again she had to qualify that slightly by writing: "(at least, some cold and close-built bower)"; in her poem "The Fish," when she wrote the words "his lower lip," she had to wonder "if you could call it a lip." Before she could allow the mountains in "Arrival at Santos" to be "self-pitying," she had to impose the words "who knows?"; in "The Armadillo," when she mentioned "the stars," she had to correct herself to say "planets, that is"; in "Sandpiper," she wrote:

> He runs, he runs straight through it, watching
>   his toes.
>
> —Watching, rather, the spaces of sand
>   between them,
> where (no detail too small) the Atlantic drains
> rapidly backwards and downwards. As he runs,
> he stares at the dragging grains.

So, too, in her poem "Trouvée" about a white hen run over on West 4th Street, she was forced to make clear that the hen, while once white, was (or is) "red-and-white now, of course." In "Poem," when she used the word "visions," she instantly wanted to change it: "'visions' is / too serious a word"; she found a calmer word: "our looks, two looks." In "The End of March," she wanted to retire and "do *nothing*, / or nothing much, forever, in two bare rooms." In one of her last poems, "Santarém," she mentioned a church twice and had to correct herself each time. The first time it is "the Cathedral, rather," and the second it is also a "Cathedral," in parentheses, but with an exclamation mark.

This urge to correct herself also appeared in her letters. In 1973, for example, she wrote to Robert Lowell: "James Merrill and I gave a joint reading—no, a sequential reading—at the YMHA."

This enacting of a search for further precision and further care with terms in the poems (and maybe in the letters too) was, in one way, a trick, a way of making the reader believe and trust a voice, or a way of quietly asking the reader to follow the poem's casual and then deliberate efforts to be faithful to what it saw, or what it knew. The trick established limits, exalted precision, made the bringing of things down to themselves into a sort of conspiracy with the reader. But she also worried about anything that might be overlooked ("no detail too small"), or not noticed properly, or exaggerated, or let too loose into grand feelings, which were not fully to be trusted. In that first poem, "The Map," Bishop seemed to disapprove of the moment when the map's printer experienced "the same excitement / as when emotion too far exceeds its cause." She was careful, or as careful as she could be, not to allow that to happen in her life or, more accurately, in her poems.

One of Me

The sense that we are only ourselves and that other people feel the same way—that they too are only themselves—is a curious thought. It is so obviously true that it is barely worth mentioning. Most people seem happier constructing other ideas that mask this basic one.

In notes he made in August 1880, Gerard Manley Hopkins considered the idea of the solitary self:

> When I consider my selfbeing; my consciousness and feeling of myself, that taste of myself, of *I* and *me* above and in all things, which is more distinctive than the taste of ale or alum, more distinctive than the smell of walnutleaf or camphor, and is incommunicable by any means to another man (as when I was a child I used to ask myself: What must it be to be someone else?). Nothing else in nature comes near this unspeakable stress of pitch, distinctiveness, and selving, this selfbeing of my own. Nothing explains it or resembles it, except so far as this, that other men to themselves have the same feeling. But this only multiplies the phenomena to be

explained so far as the cases are like and do resemble. But to me there is no resemblance: searching nature I taste *self* but at one tankard, that of my own being.

For Elizabeth Bishop too, the idea of the lone self, the single eye, the single voice, the single memory, seemed to isolate her further, especially when dramatized. It seemed to her remarkable that we are each alone. In her most openly auto-biographical essay, "The Country Mouse," published in 1961, she concluded with a memory of a first, sharp realization of her own singleness as she accompanied her aunt to the dentist's office and sat outside in the waiting room reading *National Geographic*. "A feeling of absolute and utter desolation came over me. I felt . . . *myself.* In a few days it would be my seventh birthday. I felt *I, I, I,* and looked at the three strangers in panic. I was *one* of them too, inside my scabby body and wheezing lungs."

In a poem written more than a decade later, "In the Waiting Room," she contemplated once more this first realization of her own solitary self, her single identity. In the opening of the poem, as in much of her work, she used a calm system for pretending that nothing, or nothing much, was going to happen, that she was going to stick to the known facts and add no flourishes. This is hardly poetry at all, the opening lines seemed to say, it is merely a modest statement, something that could not be disputed:

In Worcester, Massachusetts,
I went with Aunt Consuelo
to keep her dentist's appointment
and sat and waited for her
in the dentist's waiting room.

The child, as she reads the *National Geographic* magazine, is horrified by the photographs of naked black women until she is distracted by the sound of her aunt in the dentist's chair crying out. For a second she begins to believe that the cry is coming not from the aunt but actually from her ("Without thinking at all / I was my foolish aunt"). Then slowly it occurs to her that she is not her aunt, but herself:

But I felt: you are an *I*,
you are an *Elizabeth*,
you are one of *them*.
Why should you be one, too?

This realization at the age of seven seems to her strange indeed:

I knew that nothing stranger
had ever happened, that nothing
stranger could ever happen.

The strangeness was the realization of the
solitary nature of the self, of our identity and our
destiny as single and separate. This was something obvious to the world but utterly odd to the
child and, by implication, to the poet writing
more than fifty years later: "How—I didn't know
any / word for it—how 'unlikely' . . ."

"In the Waiting Room" appeared as the first
poem in Bishop's final book of poems, *Geography III*, and was followed by another, longer
meditation on the solitary self, on solitude at its
most intense. This poem, called "Crusoe in England," had echoes of Bishop's own experience.
By now, she had two landscapes to remember—
Nova Scotia, where she grew up, and Brazil,
where she had lived for many years and had now
left. The poem deals with Crusoe's remembered
solitude, a solitude recalled from a position of
an even greater, stranger solitude, that of being
alive in a populated England.

In the poem, Crusoe remembers his island:

The sun set in the sea; the same odd sun
rose from the sea,

and there was one of it and one of me.
The island had one kind of everything . . .

In this solitary space, filled with singleness, the narrator remembers poems he has read, but there are blanks, including a crucial word in Wordsworth's poem "Daffodils":

"They flash upon that inward eye,
which is the bliss . . ." The bliss of what?
One of the first things that I did
When I got back was look it up.

The word, of course, is "solitude."
Toward the end of the poem, the rescue of Crusoe is rendered starkly, in an iambic pentameter line whose rhythm is singing, almost silly, suggesting inconsequentiality, but with an undertone that is almost melancholy: "And then one day they came and took us off."

And now, no longer captive on an island, no longer living in isolation, Crusoe is imprisoned within the self, within a place where other people intrude: "Now I live here, another island, / that doesn't seem like one, but who decides?"

His knife, which held such meaning while he was alone, now seems utterly useless. It, too, is totally alone:

Now it won't look at me at all.
The living soul has dribbled away.
My eyes rest on it and pass on.

These poems by Bishop are full of resigned tones and half-resigned undertones, but there is always something else there in the space between the words, something that is controlled but not fully, so that the chaos or the panic held in check is all the more apparent because it is consigned to the shadows.

In the Village

The modest house in Great Village, Nova Scotia, where Bishop spent some of her childhood still stands in a strange costal flatness, with deep inlets all around. It is as though the whole place could be inundated by the tides at any time. If the village is built on dry land, there is a suggestion that it was not always dry, or its dryness comes as a sort of accident, a quirk of nature. The place is filled with watery northern light, which Bishop described in her poem "The Moose"; it is a place of

> . . . long tides
> where the bay leaves the sea
> twice a day and takes
> the herrings long rides,
>
> where if the river
> enters or retreats
> in a wall of brown foam
> depends on if it meets
> the bay coming in,
> the bay not at home.

The house of Bishop's grandparents, later an artists' retreat, has an air of comfort and ease and warmth. Bishop captures some of this in her poem "Sestina," where "the old grandmother / sits in the kitchen with the child," but there is also a sadness in the poem, something that cannot be easily mentioned as the grandmother is "reading the jokes from the almanac, / laughing and talking to hide her tears."

What is not mentioned in the poem is that Bishop's father died when she was eight months old, and when she was five her mother was incarcerated in a mental hospital and never saw her again. As Bishop grew older and moved away, the village in Nova Scotia and the landscape around it became a place for her of longing, of dreams. She wrote directly about what happened to her as a child not in poems, however (although what happened is buried between the words of poems, sometimes surfacing obliquely), but in two prose pieces, "In the Village" and "The Country Mouse." In the first of these, everything that happened, everything she saw in the village, is given equal weight by the child almost as a way of avoiding the idea that her mother's scream will not stop echoing in the landscape and in her memory: "The scream hangs there like that, unheard, in the memory—in the past, in the present, and those years between. It was not even loud to begin with, perhaps. It just came there to live, forever—not loud, just alive forever. Its pitch would be the pitch of my village."

In "The Country Mouse," Bishop writes of her move from the easygoing, casual beauty of Great Village to Worcester:

> I had been brought back unconsulted and against my wishes to the house my father had been born in, to be saved from a life of poverty and provincialism, bare feet, suet puddings, unsanitary school slates, perhaps even from the inverted r's of my mother's family. With this surprising extra set of grandparents, until a few weeks ago no more than names, a new life was about to begin. . . . I felt as if I were being kidnapped, even if I wasn't.

In Nova Scotia on the mornings when I stayed there, the tide was out so far that you could almost walk across the narrow bay to the beach on the other side. The houses around were modest, far apart from one another; the people were polite and seemed quiet and careful. I collected the key to the house where I was staying from a man called Amos, a name that appears in Bishop's poem "The Moose." On the first day, in the late afternoon, I thought some cataclysm had occurred as I heard a sudden roar of water outside. It was as though a dam had burst, or the level of the sea had finally risen high enough to engulf us all. In the matter of a few short minutes the whole bay filled up, vast amounts of water poured in. It was not like a storm breaking or a sudden shower of rain. It was faster than that, and almost violent. This was one of "the long tides" Bishop refers to in "The Moose."

The first reference to this poem occurs in a letter to Marianne Moore in 1946 about a trip from Great Village to Boston:

> I came back by bus—a dreadful trip, but it seemed most convenient at the time—we hailed it with a flashlight and a lantern as it went by the farm late at night. Early the next morning, just as it was getting light, the driver had to stop suddenly for a big cow moose who was wandering down the road. She walked away very slowly into the woods, looking at us over her shoulder. The driver said that one foggy night he had to stop while a huge bull moose came right up and smelled the engine.

Ten years after that original journey, the poem was still not written. In 1956 Bishop wrote to her Aunt Grace: "I've written a long poem about Nova Scotia. It's dedicated to you. When it's published, I'll send you a copy." Sixteen years later, the poem was finished. She wrote to Aunt Grace: "It is called 'The Moose.' (You are not the moose.)" Bishop read it at the joint Harvard-Radcliffe Phi Beta Kappa ceremony in 1972 and was later delighted when she heard one student's verdict: "as poems go—it wasn't bad." "I consider that a great compliment," she wrote to a friend.

The poem inhabits that space where Bishop is most comfortable; it begins almost cozily, using fact and statement with no comment. There is something unsettling about this system, as though it were a camera moving in a place that had been the site of some catastrophe, but the camera instead picks up tiny details and leaves out any sense of menace, or instead succeeds in filming menace by filming absence of menace, and thus manages to capture menace all the more truly and effectively.

The catastrophe will not even be implied in the six opening stanzas that make up one sentence in the poem, except in the sense that the description is so calm and brisk, the rhyme schemes so comforting and soft on the ear, the atmosphere so traditional and local, that something must happen to break all this up, but it is unclear what this breach of decorum can possibly be.

The poem almost establishes the idea of a common landscape; the experience of the bus making its way through this rural, traditional world suggests custom, ease, a sense of community. Bishop, who has not allowed herself here to become the narrator or the protagonist, now moves like a composer. It is as though she is working with slow tones and undertones as much as with melody in a minor key, allowing a cadence to enter for a second, letting it linger and stay and then fade to be replaced by a more dominant sound and then reemerge, more refined and mysterious. This requires great subtlety in the phrasing as night falls in the poem and the bus begin its long journey:

> The passengers lie back.
> Snores. Some long sighs.
> A dreamy divagation
> begins in the night,
> a gentle, auditory,
> slow hallucination. . . .

Bit by bit, a conversation from the back of the bus can be vaguely overheard. It should not matter, and maybe could become part of the inner music of the poem, or the careful detail it has been working with. It gradually becomes clear that, in the same way a camera can move from filming a scene to filming a face to filming the world as seen by the eyes in that face, the poem has moved into the core of a single sensibility. She is listening to the voices from the back of the bus:

Grandparents' voices

uninterruptedly
talking, in Eternity:
names being mentioned,
things cleared up finally;
what he said, what she said,
who got pensioned;

deaths, deaths and sicknesses;
the year he remarried;
the year (something) happened.
She died in childbirth.
That was the son lost
when the schooner foundered.

These overheard voices become again the voices of home, the voices of a home remembered. The poem moves from the voices of grandparents to the voices on the bus and back again in the same way that a phrase moves from being played by a single violin, to a viola, to a cello, then to a second violin, then two, and then three, and then all four of the instruments, not one of them forgetting their own solitary role in the quartet, their way of standing apart as much as playing in harmony or in unison.

And then, as though a wind instrument, or a drumbeat, were to enter the equation: "A moose has come out of / the impenetrable wood / and stands there, looms, rather, / in the middle of the road." It would be easy to say that the moose, since this is a poem, must stand for something—the eternal, say, or the disruptive in nature, or the mystery of things—other than being a mere moose. But it resists the idea that it stands for something. Rather, it *is* something. It is another part of the specific night in question, and haunting, among other reasons, because of the precise way it stayed in the memory. In other words, it is not an easy metaphor; it is hardly a metaphor at all. (Or a symbol, for that matter.) Emphatically, it is a moose before it is a metaphor, and indeed for a good while afterward.

These are late poems, and many of them deal with memory. They are not concerned to resolve anything, or offer a nostalgic picture of something in the past, but they are made, rather, as Dutch paintings of the seventeenth century were made. In 1954 Bishop recorded receiving a book of Vermeer reproductions in Brazil, and a year later wrote to the poet and critic Randall Jarrell, who had compared her poems to the paintings of Vermeer: "It has been one of my dreams that someday someone would think of Vermeer, without my saying it first, so now I think I can die in a fairly peaceful frame of mind."

In the Dutch paintings, something is made that is both real and filled with detail, but, in the play of light and shadow, in the placing of people and things, in the making of figures, it is also totally suggestive, without any of the suggestions being easy or obvious. In the same way, the devious power of these late poems by Bishop comes from what is said and what lies beneath; they use exact detail to contain emotion, and suggest more, and then leave the reader unsure, unsettled.

One of the most ambitious late poems, which seems one of the least ambitious, is called "The End of March," a poem almost loose in its tonality. It describes an aimless walk along a beach, and it has currents of aimlessness in its structure as well as undercurrents that are sharp and direct and focused. It begins in Bishop's usual casual mode, as though nothing much is going to be said: "It was cold and windy, scarcely the day / to take a walk on that long beach."

She goes on then, as though to describe her own method: "Everything was withdrawn as far as possible, / indrawn." The picture she draws of the beach and the seascape has an oddly intense melancholy, despite the casual diction. Rather than Vermeer now, it seems that the presiding spirit is more that of Cézanne, or a northern version of Cézanne, with part of the surface left blank, or like the Danish painter Vilhelm Hammershøi with much that is gray or muted, much that is filled with bareness, absence. Phrase after phrase in the poem adds up to something mysteriously beyond the phrases, or within them, pulling the eye, or perhaps the mind, in toward a desolate, almost alien scenery:

the tide far out, the ocean shrunken,
seabirds in ones or twos.
The rackety, icy, offshore wind

numbed our faces on one side;
disrupted the formation
of a lone flight of Canada geese;
and blew back the low, inaudible rollers
in upright, steely mist.

There are poems in which Bishop ponders, as Jonathan Swift did, our size in the universe, how small we are, or maybe how large, depending on the occasion and the perspective. In her early poem "The Man-Moth," for example, "the whole shadow of Man is only as big as his hat"; in "Crusoe in England":

I'd think that if they were the size
I thought volcanoes should be, then I had
become a giant;
and if I had become a giant,
I couldn't bear to think what size
the goats and turtles were,
or the gulls, or the overlapping rollers . . .

In "12 O'Clock News," the poem takes us through each small object on a desk—a lamp, for example, or a typewriter, or an ashtray—and proposes that these are large phenomena in a military landscape, to be observed with attention, and noted with fearful care.

Now, in "The End of March," there are signs on the sand that seem much larger than they should be, prints from the paw of a dog "so big / they were more like lion-prints," and there are "lengths and lengths, endless, of wet white string" whose origin is mysterious, perhaps a kite string with no kite in evidence. It is clear from the dedication that the poet is with two other people, but as always with Bishop, that idea of company is not there to be celebrated, or even taken for granted, it is there to be questioned, wondered about, and then quietly dismissed or undermined.

In the third stanza, she allows us to know that it is "I" rather than "we" who wants to "get as far as my proto-dream-house, / my crypto-dream-house" along that inhospitable beach: "I'd like to retire there and do *nothing*, / or nothing much, forever, in two bare rooms."

There is as much self-mockery here as there is sadness, as much irony as resignation; the varied meter of the two lines establishes the unsettled tone. This is a voice speaking; it is also a mind in reverie. It is both casual and deliberate; it is both whimsical and resigned.

But for Bishop, such a dream house will turn out to be disappointing, or not there. In this poem the dream house is "perfect! But—impossible." In fact the house is not even seen on that day in March:

> And that day the wind was much too cold
> even to get that far,
> and of course the house was boarded up.

And then she ends the poem with an image of the sun as a lion:

> —a sun who'd walked the beach the last low
>   tide,
> making those big, majestic paw-prints,
> who perhaps had batted a kite out of the sky
>   to play with.

This idea of the mythic figure of power, who can decide on life and death almost on a whim and in one gesture, appears again in an unpublished poem called "A Short, Slow Life," of which Bishop wrote many drafts in the late 1950s:

> We lived in a pocket of Time.
> It was close, it was warm.
> Along the dark seam of the river
> the houses, the barns, the two churches,
> hid like white crumbs
> in a fluff of gray willows and elms,

till Time made one of his gestures;
his nails scratched the shingled roof.
Roughly his hand reached in,
and tumbled us out.

The image of Time reaching into a house and tumbling out its inhabitants is a forceful and aggressive one. Bishop was uneasy about force; she had seen enough of it, perhaps. She did not publish the poem. In another poem written in Brazil around the same time, she moved more gently toward the idea that Time would not relent. In this poem, "Song for the Rainy Season," she describes the beautiful setting for the modern house where she and her partner, Lota de Macedo Soares, lived on a hillside in Petrópolis; she details the natural world with relish and care and allows "the milk-white sunrise" to be "kind to the eyes." But her wounded sensibility will relish these things only as a prelude, and in what follows she will use all her skill as a poet, all her ability to withhold and then suggest, and the move further and closer toward the truth of her own loss and her own solitude as merely preludes in themselves for the final loss, the final solitude:

For a later
era will differ.

(O difference that kills,
or intimidates, much
of all our small shadowy
life!) Without water

the great rock will stare
unmagnetized, bare,
no longer wearing
rainbows or rain,
the forgiving air
and the high fog gone;
the owls will move on
and the several
waterfalls shrivel
in the steady sun.

The Art of Losing

I come from a house where Time's hand had also reached in. Toward the end of 1963, when I was eight, in the town of Enniscorthy in the southeast of Ireland, I arrived home from school one day to find both of my parents standing still, looking into a mirror. My father, my mother said, would have to have an operation. She spoke, I remember, both to myself and to the mirror, and, of course, to my father, who was looking at her in the mirror as she spoke, as I was. Between then and sometime later—four, maybe five, months—myself and my brother, who was four, were looked after by an aunt a good distance away, and we did not see our parents or hear anything about them. They were in Dublin. We knew that. He was in hospital.

When I saw my father again, he was sitting in a chair in a corner in another aunt's house back in the town. He had an enormous gash on the side of his head, a wound that looked as though it had been badly stitched, the flesh stretched to where the stitching had been done. He had had a brain operation. When he stood up, I saw that he had to walk slowly, with effort. I don't remember him speaking then, but soon I realized I could not understand him when he spoke, nor could anybody, except with difficulty.

By then, I had developed my own problems with speech. I am not sure when it began, if it was in the time before my brother and I went to stay with my aunt, or while we were there, or when we came back, but sometime in 1964 I developed a stammer that could often be very bad. I could not begin a sentence with a hard consonant. My own name was a special nightmare. I could not say either of my names if anyone asked me. I would do everything I could, but the sounds would not come. Even today, I still have to be careful with my breathing if anyone asks me my name. Years later, in a casual conversation, I learned that I was once taken to the speech therapist whom my father also used, but I must have begun all sentences with soft sounds, and she did not think there was any problem.

I have a close relationship with silence, with things withheld, things known and not said. I am sure that no one said anything to me, for example, before I went into that room where I saw my father after the operation. And no one mentioned afterward that we would not easily be able to understand his speech, and that my speech was also a problem. What was there to say? And we lived like that for three and a half years; we got used to it. And then in July 1967 my father died. There was a funeral and the house was full of people, but there was silence again soon afterward. My other siblings went away, back to what they were doing. My younger brother and I stayed there with my mother. We thought about my father, or we did sometimes, but we did not talk about him.

Six weeks after his death, I enrolled as a student in the school where he had been a teacher. Almost immediately, in that September of 1967, I discovered poetry. In the front room of our small house, as I was meant to be studying science or Latin, I was reading poetry. I read some of the early poems by Yeats over and over, and then I read anything else I could find. My mother had some poetry books and anthologies. She had written and published poems before her marriage. *The Penguin Book of Contemporary Verse* was in the house, and through this I found poems by W. H. Auden, Louis Mac-Neice, William Empson, Thom Gunn, Sylvia Plath. Soon, I had a copy of *The New Poetry*, an anthology edited by A. Alvarez, with even more poems by Plath and Gunn. I checked out a hardback copy of Auden's *City Without Walls* from the library and devoured it. I also began to write poems myself—the first was about a tree in a landscape with no other trees around—and I found a magazine run by the Capuchin order called *Eirigh,* and they began to accept and print some of the poems I wrote; they sent me postal orders for small amounts of money. I told no one about this, so I was shocked and ashamed when an uncle found the magazine and saw my name and then showed the printed poem to all the family.

At fifteen, when I was going to boarding school, I was told that I would not be able to bring books other than schoolbooks. So I spent the month of August 1970 copying out poems by hand into notebooks so that I would have them with me. During a trip to Dublin, on one of those Christmas holidays, I bought Sylvia Plath's *Ariel* and Seamus Heaney's *Death of a Naturalist.* By the time I went to university in 1972, I certainly knew some poems by Robert Lowell, and through them in turn had come across the name of Elizabeth Bishop. I know that I bought her *Selected Poems*, published by Chatto and Windus, in the Compendium Bookshop on Camden High Street in London during the Easter break of 1975, when I was nineteen.

It seems strange now that the poem by her that I liked best then and learned by heart was "Cirque d'Hiver," a poem about a "mechanical toy," a poem with elaborate rhyme schemes and a tone close to a nursery rhyme.

> Across the floor flits the mechanical toy,
> fit for a king of several centuries back.
> A little circus horse with real white hair.
> His eyes are glossy black.
> He bears a little dancer on his back.

The poem seems so determined to be jolly and inconsequential, almost jokey, that it is hard to find the undertow in it, which arises oddly from the sheer amount of time and energy spent observing this scene in such great and good-humored detail to the exclusion of all else. Somehow I felt a sense that, in concentrating on this and this only and for a long time, the poem hinted that the rest of the world could be kept away and made to seem not to matter. By the end of the poem, in any case, the dancer on the horse who has a "little pole / that pierces both her body and her soul" has turned her back on us, and the poet catches the eye of the horse:

> Facing each other rather desperately—
> his eye is like a star—

we stare and say, "Well, we have come this
far."

I carried Bishop's *Selected Poems* in my red
suitcase when I went to Barcelona in September
1975. It had become a treasured book. I liked the
idea, I suppose, that Bishop had traveled, which I
was doing now, and I noticed a tone that avoided
easy or obvious drama. She used detail and shifts
of tone to suggest feeling, to conceal feeling, and
perhaps mask feeling. And this meant something
to me then, as it still does. Bishop also wrote
about the sea; and we had spent all our summers
close to the sea in a place called Ballyconnigar
Upper, or Cush, in the southeast of Ireland. Dublin, where I had gone to university, was also on
the sea. Barcelona, too, was on the sea, as other
cities where I would live, such as Buenos Aires
and San Francisco, would also be on the sea, as
the room where I am writing this overlooks the
Hudson River, which at times seems to be flowing the wrong way because of the tides.

As soon as I had been in Barcelona for a few
days, I realized that I wanted to stay there and
live there. I felt sometimes that I had escaped.
I had found a replacement for home; I would,
I thought, not have to think again much about
what had happened at home. The marl of the

cliffs at Ballyconnigar and the muted gray colors of clouds over the sea there seemed dull indeed compared to the glamour of the Mediterranean. The life I found in the new city, so filled with bright distraction, was far away from the house where I was brought up, and distant indeed from the loss, the silence.

I had also escaped Ireland in 1975, with its dull and controlling Catholicism, its political conservatism, its intractable historical problems emerging again in the guise of car bombs, armed struggles, nationalism. I had come, of course, to the wrong country if I wanted to find a private world. Within two months of my arrival in Spain, General Franco died and the public realm entered all our lives like a rushing, incoming tide. Catalan nationalism became a strange, mirror image of Irish nationalism. The legacy of the Spanish civil war was part of daily life. In my first novel, *The South*, I wrote about a woman coming from Ireland to Barcelona in the 1950s in search of a place where history would not matter to her, only to find that history leaves strange and insistent traces, only to find that history would come to blight privacy all the more fiercely because of the original urge to escape the sound of ancestral voices.

In the summer of 1983, as I was working on that novel in a hotel room in the Algarve region of Portugal, I came to an impasse. The two main characters had followed my trajectory; they had left Enniscorthy and landed in Barcelona, where they had lived. I had written chapters about the enigma of arrival, about the excitement of the new city, and then about settling there, and also about a sort of unsettlement that came with being away from your own country in a new place of choice. I had written my chapters on the legacy of the civil war in Catalonia. But the novel wasn't finished; it needed something else, but I had no idea what. I remembered what the Irish painter Barrie Cooke had said to me about starting a painting; he said "you just make a mark." I was working on a manual typewriter. I thought I would close my eyes for a while, think of nothing, open them and type a word, any word, and then see where that word led. I wrote: "The sea." And then I wrote: "A grey shine on the sea."

Suddenly, I was back in an Irish landscape, with Irish weather, and not only that, but in a very precise place—the strand at Ballyconnigar on the Wexford coast. I moved my characters there, and I found a calm, stable, melancholy tone to work with. I could see the shore stretching south to Curracloe in many types of Irish summer weather, including days when the haze so easily becomes mist and when soft clouds so easily darken and become rain. Somehow, writing about it was easier than writing about Spain, and the sentences came with less strain.

I was surprised. While I had regularly been back in Enniscorthy, which was ten miles inland from Ballyconnigar, to see my family, I had not thought that this world was something I could write about. It belonged to me so fundamentally that I saw no drama in it; also, it was a place of loss, and I was, although I did not put a name on it then, in flight from loss. In *The South*, nonetheless, I wrote about loss; it was not something that would ever leave me, but I had set it in another landscape, one as far away from the original site of pain as I could get.

With this novel, I had begun with thoughts about sex and glamour and art, and I ended up writing about exile and grief. In the novel that came next, I set out to write about politics and history, but it became a story about inner exile and grief, set firmly on that stretch of Irish coast.

I did not plan what happened then, how the novel I wrote next was set in Buenos Aires, where

I had lived in 1985, to be followed by a novel set once more on that coastline in Ireland and also, for the first time, in the very house where I was brought up. A pattern began—escape, return, escape, return—that I could not easily control.

I remember arriving in Halifax, Nova Scotia, to do a reading in 2008, having flown that day from San Francisco; I remember moving from a warm spring into a place where there was ice in the air, and feeling sharp relief that I was in the brisk climate where I belonged, that the attempt to escape this cold spring had been a sojourn whose substance crumbled now as I breathed the cold northern air, almost familiar. But the opposite happened too. It happened on golden mornings in San Francisco, mornings when I felt that just looking at the way things grew and the soft exquisite light would be enough, that because of the sheer sweet intensity in how nature greeted my eyes, I would never want anything else.

Novels and stories only come for me when an idea, a memory, or an image move into rhythm. This happens almost of its own accord, and the work can only happen when the initial impulse and the rhythm become nearly inseparable. In the past thirty years as I worked on fiction, the impulse and the rhythm have pulled me away from home—Spain, Argentina, the United States, the Holy Land—and then have also nudged me, forced me, pulled me, dragged me, back home to the damp air and the dulled light of the southeast of Ireland, closer and closer to things that happened there, to the place of loss, to the loss itself, to minute details, to the very spaces.

Thus when I read Elizabeth Bishop's final book, *Geography III*, poems that dealt with such care and precision with Nova Scotia, her place of loss, poems that dealt with the pull toward a place despite the lure of elsewhere, I saw something that I knew and felt. I read *Geography III* in 1978, the year after it came out, the year when I had returned to Ireland from Spain. I was twenty-three and had stopped writing poetry. I did not know then that Bishop's poetics of north and south, home and elsewhere, would haunt me and nourish the work I would do in fiction. But I was interested in her tone, by the suggestions of loss, by her way of making what was unfamiliar seem even stranger, and during my first journey to Brazil in 1985, I had her on my mind and in my sights.

Nature Greets Our Eyes

I stayed for a while in the spring of 1985 in a narrow street near the Flamingo Park in Rio de Janeiro and went out some days to swim at Copacabana. It was that time between the death of Elizabeth Bishop and the appearance of the first biography and *One Art*, a volume of her letters, a time when the ordinary reader knew very little about her. I did not know, for example, that for fifteen years she had lived periodically in an apartment overlooking the beach at Copacabana. "It is such a wonderful apartment," she wrote to Robert Lowell in 1958, "that we'll never rent it again, no matter what heights rents soar to, I think. Top floor, 11th, a terrace around two sides, overlooking all that famous bay and beach. Ships go by all the time, like targets in a shooting gallery, people walk their dogs—same dogs same time, same old man in blue trunks every morning with two Pekinese at 7 a.m.—and at night the lovers on the mosaic sidewalks cast enormous long shadows over the soiled sand."

I remember the shock of the first Saturday I was there, how there were dozens of football matches being played with extraordinary speed and ferocity on the beach, most of the players beautiful, the supporters letting off firecrackers every time a goal was scored, and the firecrackers echoing against the apartment blocks and hotels. They played until it grew dark, and then another drama began. In her book *Brazil*, written with the editors of *Life* magazine, Bishop wrote: "Frequently at night, on country roads, along beaches or in city doorways, candles can be seen glimmering. A black candle, cigars, and a black bottle of cachaça, or a white candle, white flowers, a chicken and a clear bottle of cachaça—these are macumba hexes or offerings, witnesses to the superstitious devotion of millions of Brazilians to this cult."

I watched a woman in her forties kneeling at the edge of the sea and a girl who must have been her daughter. They had left red roses on the sand and lit several candles around the roses. They had left a glass of alcohol on the sand. The firecrackers and the shouting from the football matches were over now, a faint memory. The two women were facing out to sea, watching the gray waves come in, wringing their hands in desperate concentration.

This is the space in which the best of Bishop's poems survived. She conjured up what Robert Lowell in his 1947 review of *North & South* called "something in motion, weary but persisting," and then moved to something exact and specific, something purely human and fragile, what Lowell identified as "rest, sleep, fulfillment, or death." Bishop delighted in the exotic, in the passing, noisy, frivolous moment, but in the end her eye was always caught by something else; her eye would have caught the flame and the woman kneeling by the sea. In "Apartment in Leme," an unpublished poem from 1969, she wrote about the beach as viewed from her apartment in the morning:

> white candles with wet, blackened wicks,
> and green glass bottles for white alcohol
> meant for the goddess meant to come last night.

In 1985 when I stayed in Rio, however, I did not know much more about Bishop than she told us in her poems, the short biography in her books and the shadowy figure described in Ian Hamilton's biography of Robert Lowell, which appeared in 1983. In that same year Denis Donoghue, in a new edition of his *Connoisseurs of Chaos*, wrote:

> Elizabeth Bishop was born in Worcester, Massachusetts, on February 8, 1911. Her father

died when she was eight months old. Her mother, mentally ill, spent long periods in hospital; she was taken, when Elizabeth was five, to a mental hospital in Dartmouth, Nova Scotia. Elizabeth never saw her again. The child was brought up partly by her grandparents in Nova Scotia, partly by her mother's older sister in Boston. When she was sixteen, she went to a boarding school near Boston, and from there to Vassar College. . . . From 1938 she spent ten years in Key West, Florida. In 1942 she met, in New York, a Brazilian, Lota Costallat de Macedo Soares, and, beginning in 1951, they shared a house near Petrópolis in Brazil, and an apartment in Rio de Janeiro. Bishop wrote a book about Brazil, and stayed there for fifteen years, writing her poems and translating some poetry by modern Brazilian poets. In 1966 she returned to the United States, teaching poetry at various universities and especially at Harvard; in 1974 she took an apartment in Boston. She died in the winter of 1979. So far as appearances go, her life was not dramatic. But one never knows about drama.

There was, however, one piece of evidence that suggested drama. In 1970 Robert Lowell published "Four Poems for Elizabeth Bishop" in *Notebook*. The first was a reworking of his poem "Water"; the second poem was more obscure, containing several personal references; the third was called "Letter with Poems for a Letter with Poems." It began: "'You're right to worry about me, only please DON'T, / though I'm pretty worried myself. I've somehow got / into the worst situation I've ever / had to cope with.'" It included the lines: "'That's what I feel I'm waiting for now: / a faintest glimmer I am going to get out / somehow alive from this.'"

The fourth poem ended with Lowell's homage to Bishop as an artist. In *Notebook,* they read: "Do / you still hang words in air, ten years imperfect, / joke-letters, glued to cardboard posters, with gaps / and empties for the unimagined phrase, / unerring Muse who scorns a less casual friendships?" In *History*, published three years later, Lowell improved the lines: "Do / you still hang your words in air, ten years / unfinished, glued to your notice board, with gaps / or empties for the unimaginable phrase—/ unerring Muse who makes the casual perfect?"

These lines seemed reasonable: Bishop's poems were full of unimaginable phrases, there was a calm austerity in her tone, which could lead readers to feel that she worked for years on each poem. She sought a quiet perfection, which was remarkable at a time when such contemporaries as Lowell and Berryman were writing unending and imperfect sequences. But the tone of the third poem, in which Lowell had seemed to quote from a letter of hers, seemed strange, a dramatic, personal, and highly charged tone that had never entered into Bishop's poetry and seemed closer to Lowell's own work. It was Bishop's calm voice turned shrill.

The tone of this sonnet seemed to be an affront to the sense of pain and loss buried deep in her poetic diction. She would never have allowed such easy drama into her poems. Instead, she used a peculiar and steadfast concentration, which could allow certain forms of heightened rhetoric to come to the surface only infrequently, and then after much preparatory work had been done. This rhetoric is at its most powerful, for example, in the last part of her poem "At the Fishhouses":

If you should dip your hand in,
your wrist would ache immediately,
your bones would begin to ache and your
    hand would burn
as if the water were a transmutation of fire

that feeds on stones and burns with a dark
gray flame.

Bishop shared with Hemingway a fierce simplicity, a use of words in which the emotion seems to be hidden, seems to lurk mysteriously in the space between. The search for pure accuracy in her poems forced Bishop to watch the world helplessly, as though there was nothing she could do. The statements she made in her poems seem always distilled, put down—despite the simplicity and the tone of casual directness—on the page only with great difficulty. Her poem "The Prodigal," for example, comes in the shape of two sonnets. The first one ends: "And then he thought he almost might endure / his exile yet another year or more." The second ends: "But it took him a long time / finally to make his mind up to go home." The first ending hints at infinite regret and resignation in the "almost endure" rhyming with "another year or more." As a poet, Bishop stole a great deal from the sound of prose, as a painter might steal from photography. She made the last line of the poem seem casual and uncertain, as though nothing was happening, nothing poetic, but maybe something all the more real and exact and affecting for that. She left "finally" at the beginning of the line like an awkward prose word against the sure-footed iambics of "to make his mind up to go home." But the extraordinary amount of emotion in so many of her lines seemed to derive not so much from her skill as a poet (although from that too) but from a repressed desperation and anxiety that filled the air in her poems, a sense of a hurt and wounded personality which sought to remain clear-eyed and calm—"awful but cheerful," in her own phrase, the phrase that ended her poem "The Bight" and also appears on her gravestone ("ALL THE UNTIDY ACTIVITY CONTINUES, AWFUL BUT CHEERFUL").

In 1964 she wrote to Robert Lowell about the poetry of Philip Larkin: "Larkin's poetry is a bit too easily resigned to grimness don't you think? Oh, I am all for grimness and horrors of every sort—but you can't have them, either, by short-cuts—by just saying it." "Grimness and horrors of every sort" remain unsaid and unspoken in most of her work. What was in between the lines of her poems was allowed to speak for itself. "What one seems to want in art, in experiencing it, is the same thing that is necessary for its creation, a self-forgetful, perfectly useless concentration," she wrote, or "I have a vague theory that one learns most—I have learned most—from having someone suddenly make fun of something one has taken seriously up until then. I mean about life, the world, and so on."

Some of Bishop's letters throw soft light on the poems. In "Poem," she describes a painting done by her great-uncle George and suddenly realizes that she knew the place he painted, she had been there too. "Heavens, I recognize the place, I know it!" the poem reads. It is risky to use a word like "heavens," especially if the poet is worried, as Bishop must have been, about being precious and whimsical. The rest of the poem is more hard and exact, but the reader is still entitled to puzzle why "heavens" was used. Bishop's letters make clear that "Heavens" was part of her natural style, her own voice. It comes up at many times in her letters. ("Heavens, it will be nice to carry on an all-English conversation again"; "Heavens, how I hate politics after the last four years"; "Heavens, what a vale of tears it is"; "Oh heavens, now John Ashbery and I have to go and have an 'intimate' lunch with Ivar Ivask.")

Similarly, readers of her poem "The End of March" will find echoes in several of the letters. "And then I've always had a daydream," she wrote to Robert Lowell in l960, "of being a lighthouse keeper, absolutely alone, with no one to interrupt my reading or just sitting." Three years later, in another letter to Lowell, she wrote: "Then I joined [Lota] up there and we spent two whole weeks doing nothing much."

But clues come too from the landscape of Nova Scotia itself and from the way people speak there. One early morning, while staying south of Halifax in 2010, as I listened to the local radio station, I heard the announcer express surprise. "Heavens," she said, before she explained what had surprised her. The word seemed natural, or must have seemed so to most listeners. So, too, if I drove just a few minutes down to the road and turned right back toward the coast, I came to a pier with fishhouses. I stood watching, as she must have done, a seal in the water ("One seal particularly / I have seen here evening after evening"), and then I looked at the water itself, the water that she studied during a journey back to Nova Scotia on a beach also south of Halifax in 1946 and wrote about in her notebook: "Description of the dark, icy, clear water—clear, dark glass—slightly bitter (hard to define). My idea of knowledge, this cold stream, half drawn, half flowing from a great rocky breast." Later, she rewrote her notes, transformed them for the extraordinary ending of her poem "At the Fishhouses":

> If you tasted it, it would first taste bitter,
> then briny, then surely burn your tongue.
> It is like what we imagine knowledge to be:
> dark, salt, clear, moving, utterly free,
> drawn from the cold hard mouth
> of the world, derived from the rocky breasts
> forever, flowing and drawn, and since
> our knowledge is historical, flowing, and flown.

Bishop concluded her poem "Questions of Travel" with the unanswerable question: *"Should we have stayed at home, / wherever that may be?"* She was, of course, never sure. She made her homes on a single line of longitude, or close to one: Massachusetts, Nova Scotia, New York, Key West, Rio de Janeiro, Boston. In 1976, three years before she died, she wrote: "All my life I have lived and behaved very much like that sandpiper [in her poem 'Sandpiper']— just running along the edges of different countries 'looking for something.' I have always felt I couldn't *possibly* live very far inland, away from the ocean; and I *have* always lived near it, frequently in sight of it." Like her sandpiper, she said, she had spent her life "timorously pecking for subsistence along coastlines of the world."

No matter where she was, however, she thought of elsewhere. At the end of her double-sonnet "The Prodigal," she allowed the protagonist to think that he might go home. But there is no third sonnet showing his arrival. Like Crusoe, it was easier to dream of home than to be there. At the opening of "The Moose," the theme is leaving rather than staying; the bus is departing for Boston. Bishop was more at ease, or less ill-at-ease, in exile. In an unpublished poem, written in Brazil in the mid-1960s, she looked north, away from where she was, to elsewhere where she was sure she belonged:

> Dear, my compass
> still points north
> to wooden houses
> and blue eyes

In a letter to a publisher in May 1906, another great exile, James Joyce, set out in terms both ambitious and modest what he had in mind when he composed the stories in his volume *Dubliners*: "My intention was to write a chapter of the moral history of my country and I chose Dublin for the scene because that city seemed to be the centre of paralysis. . . . I have written it for the most part in a style of scrupulous meanness and with the conviction that he is a very bold man who dares to alter in the presentment, still more to deform, whatever he has seen and heard."

Joyce began the stories in Dublin in 1904, when he was twenty-two, as he was preparing to leave his native Dublin, and finished the last one, "The Dead," in 1906 and 1907 in Trieste, where he would live until 1920 before moving to Paris. His description of his style—"scrupulous meanness," by which he meant a conscious avoidance of flourishes or bright display, a tone held back, held down—could equally be the calm, precise style that Bishop used in her poems of Nova Scotia. Both writers understood that the words themselves, if rendered precisely and exactly with no flourishes, could carry even more coiled emotion than an ornate phrase or sentences filled with elaborate textures.

Both Joyce and Bishop were working with memory and with experience lost or soon to be lost. In both cases, these two artists, throughout a long exile, sought to be exact about places. When they allowed the tone of their work to soar, there was the feeling that they had earned the right to do so by holding back so much in the pages that came before.

In her early poem "Over 2,000 Illustrations and a Complete Concordance," Bishop's tone is breezy, amused, playful, as she browses a book of illustrations. Sometimes in her work she is prepared to leave things at that, merely hinting at darker and more substantial preoccupations, or leaving the breeziness ambiguous, giving her words a day off from deep significance. But as this poem nears the end, she alerts the reader to a shift in tone: "It was somewhere near there / I saw what frightened me most of all." The description then moves into the meticulous, the highly charged. Her eye begins to note things with ferocity and concentration. The tone becomes more and more unsettled as the eye settles and examines, using pauses and repetitions:

> A holy grave, not looking particularly holy,
> one of a group under a keyhole-arched stone
>   baldaquin
> open to every wind from the pink desert.
> An open, gritty, marble trough, carved solid
> with exhortation, yellowed
> as scattered cattle-teeth;

half-filled with dust, not even the dust
of the poor prophet paynim who once lay there.

The image is stark and haunting, uncertain of itself. Its very uncertainty suggests disturbance, deals with the matter of time and decay, something that mattered once, fading, fading. The sadness, the fright are buried in the rhythm. And since this scene of what was once sacred can be examined and can yield so much, she then moves to the picture of the Nativity to find that it yields both more and less, as the poem comes to an end. Her description of her own motive here is casual, as though it were nothing: "Why couldn't we have seen / this old Nativity while we were at it?" The "while we were at it" breathes life into a dead phrase, and also suggests that nothing much now is going to happen, as a way of making the last five lines of the poem, with their hushed majesty, all the more convincing and disturbing and strange:

—the dark ajar, the rocks breaking with light,
an undisturbed, unbreathing flame,
colorless, sparkless, freely fed on straw,
and, lulled within, a family with pets,
—and looked and looked our infant sight away.

Bishop also used a tone that was rich with cadence and lifted language in her poem "At the Fishhouses" only when she had, once more, offered a description both precise and casual of the scene she was inspecting. Some of the description is almost mathematical in its exactness:

Down at the water's edge, at the place
where they haul up the boats, up the long
     ramp
descending into the water, thin silver
tree trunks are laid horizontally
across the gray stones, down and down
at intervals of four or five feet.

Toward the end of the poem, however, the tone changes. As Seamus Heaney has written: "What we have been offered, among other things, is the slow-motion spectacle of a well-disciplined poetic imagination being tempted to dare a big leap, hesitating, and then with powerful sureness actually taking the leap." The tone of the poems heightens, uses repetition, and then offers the water a slow and unearthly power: "as if the water were a transmutation of fire / that feeds on stones and burns with a dark gray flame." Then Bishop allows it, as we have seen, to stand for knowledge.

This method, the movement from very detailed and exact description to a moment that is totalizing and hallucinatory in its tone, which moves above the scene and attempts in its cadences both to wrest meaning and create further mystery from the scene below, occurs also in the very final passage of Joyce's "The Dead," which, in describing the snow, also takes a leap. The tone moves away from "scrupulous meanness" and a suspicion of beauty, using cadence and repetition:

It was falling on every part of the dark central plain, on the treeless hills, falling softly upon the Bog of Allen and further westward, softly falling into the dark mutinous Shannon waves. It was falling, too, upon every part of the lonely churchyard on the hill where Michael Furey lay buried. It lay thickly drifted on the crooked crosses and headstones, on the spears of the little gate, on the barren thorns. His soul swooned slowly as he heard the snow falling faintly through the universe and faintly falling, like the descent of their last end, upon all the living and the dead.

In "The Dead," Joyce allows the protagonist to live in internal exile. Gabriel attends the party in his aunts' house, but he does not feel involved. He stands and watches, rather than participates. And in the moment when he attempts to join in what others are doing—the dancing—it is made clear to him by an old friend, Miss Ivors, that the very language he speaks and writes in— English—may not even *be* his language. Miss Ivors believes that the proper language for Irish people is Gaelic and not English, and the place they must visit in order to become fully attuned to the self at its most pure is not Europe, or even Dublin, but the Aran Islands off the west coast of Ireland. The encounter leaves Gabriel uneasy, and this is a preparation for the scene with his wife when he will realize that he has never really known her, that he is not merely a stranger in society, and perhaps in his own country, but also in his own marriage. He does not need to travel to feel homesick; there is no home.

This is, however, merely a beginning, just as Bishop's witnessing as a helpless observer in her poem "At the Fishhouses," someone merely visiting with a notebook a landscape that may be home, but may also be lost, is merely the beginning of something, the mere setting of a scene. It is not enough. Both Gabriel's alienation in "The Dead" and Bishop's ability to observe minutely in "At the Fishhouses" offer a problem in both the story and the poem. No homecoming is allowed, no lifting of the isolation. Instead, another form of lifting, which is oddly open-ended, appears at the end of the story and the poem.

Neither James Joyce nor Elizabeth Bishop returned to live their lives in Dublin or Nova Scotia. What they did more than anything else was remember, visualize. It was essential for them that the remembering be exact and precise, enough for it to draw in and hold all the emotions surrounding belonging, or dreams of belonging, or loss, or dreams of loss, or indeed knowledge of loss. This, then, allowed Joyce to release a soaring energy when it was required at the end of "The Dead" and Bishop too at the end of "At the Fishhouses." They could allow language to compensate and console, then rise above such petty urges and seem to redeem what had been lost, or redress much that they both cared about deeply. The eye and the voice moved into a space that was impersonal, beyond the personal, and then they allowed this impersonality to transform everything that lay beneath it or beyond its understanding, creating a music filled with risk and repetition, which would mimic the tones of prayer, the mind at its most exalted.

It matters, I think, that both writers are dealing with northern light, northern weather. Ireland and Nova Scotia have their inhospitable seasons and their barren hinterlands; they are places where the light is often scarce and the memory of poverty is close; they are places in which the spirit is wary and the past comes haunting and much is unresolved. Mist, wind, clouds, short days, the proximity of the sea, the quickly changing weather, all suggest a world in which little can be taken for granted. In *Dubliners*, Joyce created a tone for that scarcity, as Bishop did in many of her poems about Nova Scotia.

In Joyce's Irish Catholic world and in the beliefs of Bishop's Baptist upbringing, the relationship to God is stark, almost simple. When faith disappears, as it did with these two writers, then the language of transcendence can have a special power because it invokes something that was once familiar, once possible, and is now lost.

Faith goes; language remains. Slowly, the new faithless language takes on a power much greater than it ever had when it was there merely to express faith. Language is all there is now. And in the ambiguous space created by a precise and exact evocation of the past, a single, concluding image—the image of the snow in Joyce and the quasireligious images of water in Bishop—is allowed to soar above the ordinary universe like a hymn, or an aria, something filled with rising cadence. This image offers a completion (or a tentative, sonorous reaching toward completion) that is mysterious, hard-won, uplifting, out-lifting, but also credible and concrete. A sort of homecoming is enacted by allowing the image to transform itself, free itself from the shackles of the concrete, the positive, the world of things, and move like a boat sent to rescue someone, into an uneasy, shimmering, almost philosophical, almost religious space, using words with both freedom and restraint, suggesting something that has not been formulated or imagined by anyone before.

Order and Disorder in Key West

Some days in Key West, the military jets shot across the blue sky over the sea; it felt as though the windows would break. It was hard not to forget that at that time America was still at war, hard not to forget that it was preparing its systems for future wars. It was January 2013. In the morning the light came all soft liquid, like something fragile rising and spreading, then becoming richer. In the streets, roosters moved freely and easily. From their perspective, if they just looked down or straight ahead, Key West belonged to them. Theirs was the first sound of the day, their cries often coming before the first light appeared.

Elizabeth Bishop came to Key West in 1938 and lived there most of the time for a decade. Her poem "Roosters," first published in 1941, set in Key West as war loomed, is a work of large, suggestive ambition and formal intricacy. The stanza system was based on "Wishes to His (Supposed) Mistress," by the seventeenth-century metaphysical poet Richard Crashaw:

Who ere she bee,
That not impossible she
That shall command my heart and mee;

Where ere she lye,
Lock't up from mortal Eye
In shady leaves of Destiny

The three lines of the first stanza of Bishop's poem have two beats, and then three, and then five; on the page the beats are emphatic, although when you hear Bishop read the poem aloud they are less so. Of the nineteen words in the first stanza of the poem (I am reading "o'clock" as two words), there is only one word with more than one syllable, and that is in the middle of a line:

At four o'clock
in the gun-metal blue dark
we hear the first crow of the first cock

The cock and the clock rhyme in a single sound; the dark, still half in place, disturbed rather than fully woken, merely gets a half-rhyme. The first stanza runs on, without any punctuation, into the second, which has two beats in the first line, three in the second and four (or five, if you include the first word "and") softer ones in the third:

just below
the gun-metal blue window
and immediately there is an echo

"Below" and "echo" don't quite rhyme since the stress is on the "low" and the "ech"; this means that the "o" in "echo" comes more as the echo of a rhyme than a full rhyme, which is also the case with "window," where the stress falls on the "wind" rather than the "o," thus the rhyme here is below the word, so to speak, rather that flat on it. The word "immediately" means what it says, but because it has five syllables when so far there have only been four words with two syllables and none with three or four syllables, the word manages to suggest time taking its time, taking a few uneasy beats, between the "crow" and the "echo," which, once more, are not fully rhyming words, but rather two words in which the unstressed syllable of the second echoes the single sound of the first.

The next stanza reads:

> off in the distance,
> then one from the backyard fence,
> then one, with horrible insistence,

"Off in the distance" is distant by a stanza from the crow whose echo it is. Since the echo is distant from what came before, the stress on the final word will be on the first syllable "dis" while the second—"tance"—will have a sound that falls off. But the next sound is closer, thus the only word in this second line with two syllables—"backyard"—will have two clear, strong beats of equal measure. The last word in this line—"fence"—will match up to the previous two sounds. Since the next sound has a "horrible insistence," the word "insistence" will have a rhyme with "distance" that is almost irritating. Those final two words will stand alone with three syllables each, going against the staccato sound of the poem, holding it up, blocking its cadence.

The next stanza, which ends the first sentence of the poem, reads:

> grates like a wet match
> from the broccoli patch,
> flares, and all over town begins to catch.

The rhyme-scream spreads in the poems as the rooster calls begin to catch. The phrase "horrible insistence" does indeed grate; its diction mirrors the sound from the broccoli patch. As this sound flares, or just before, there is a direct rhyme, a verbal flaring, between "match" and "patch." Just as "immediately" took time in this poem filled with single, urgent, sharp sounds, or flat sounds, so too now the eight syllables of "and all over town begins to" have a softer sound, they move slowly and casually to connect the two verbs with action in them, "flares" and "catch." In this stanza, the sound of the roosters has become more pervasive; for the first time the three words at the end of each line, each a word of one syllable—"match," "patch," "catch"—rhyme directly with one another. The world is awake; the next stanza can begin with conviction with the phrase "Cries galore."

It is important to insist that the poem "Roosters" is about roosters. Perhaps, more exactly, it is about roosters in Key West, since one of the final stanzas catches the strange quality of dense sea-light in the morning on the island:

> In the morning
> a low light is floating
> in the backyard, and gilding
>
> from underneath
> the broccoli, leaf by leaf;

And the poem is about roosters in Key West since roosters there dominate urban space as though they own it. It is hard not to notice them in all their arrogance:

> The crown of red
> set on your little head
> is charged with all your fighting blood.

Yet the poem was written as the navy, much to Bishop's annoyance, moved into Key West and took over land and demolished houses, and it has been read as an antiwar poem or a poem against arbitrary authority: "what right have you to give / commands and tell us how to live."

And the poem included a condemnation of a world run by men:

> Deep from protruding chests
> in green-gold medals dressed,
> planned to command and terrorize the rest,
>
> the many wives
> who lead hens' lives
> of being courted and despised.

But the poem maintains its autonomy, its pure space, despite these readings. If Bishop had wanted to write a poem about the war and maleness and militarism, she would, or might, have done so, although it would have been unlikely. Just as if she had wanted to write a poem in celebration of lesbian love, or about the end of love, she might have done so too. (Indeed, she did so in some of her earlier poems, and in "It is marvellous to wake up together," written in Key West in the same period as "Roosters," although she did not publish it; it was published after her death. She did so too in "Song for the Rainy Season," written in Brazil and published in 1960.)

By fixing "Roosters" in the real, she managed, by drawing the subject of the poem so precisely, to have the roosters enact things and possess qualities with immense suggestive power. By observing the roosters closely and meticulously, she managed a poem about power simply by exercising her own power not to overstate the case. She offered the poem a symbolic force by implication only, making it all the more powerful because of the sheer openness, the rawness, of the implications; she offered the poem a symbolic intensity by searching for an intensity within the form of the poem and within its diction. She managed to write one of the great poems about power and cruelty by not doing so, by describing, suggesting, by working on her rhythms and cadences, her rhymes and her half-rhymes, by leaving it at that, by understanding what might be enough.

In "Roosters," she also managed to produce one of the great poems about the morning. She was, as a poet, more comfortable with the arrival of morning than she was with the fall of night. She wrote many poems of waking, with tentative pale light, "a weak white sky," things beginning; she wrote aubades. As a poet, she loved the sheer openness that the morning offered a poem, and then relished dramatizing how the innocence of the morning could be disturbed and destroyed—she dramatized "the violations of the morning," in David Kalstone's wonderful phrase. The morning light in her poems was filled with erasures and would then be filled with small complexities. There was nothing except what could begin. In an early poem "Love Lies Sleeping," she began:

> Earliest morning, switching all the tracks
> that cross the sky from cinder star to star,
> coupling the ends of streets
> to trains of light,
>
> now draw us into daylight in our beds.

In other early poems such as "A Miracle for Breakfast" or "Paris, 7 A.M." she also invoked the morning with a strange and uneasy surrealism in the first, and imagery that is disturbing and filled with odd sudden moments of menace in the second. In "Anaphora," the "white-gold skies our eyes / first open on" made her wonder, "Where is the music coming from, the energy?"

"Rain Towards Morning" begins with the fierce, fleeting energy of birdsong:

> The great light cage has broken up in the air,
> freeing, I think, about a million birds
> whose wild ascending shadows will not be back

And in "Five Flights Up," Bishop found three large adjectives to describe the great morning light of Rio de Janeiro: "Enormous morning, ponderous, meticulous."

In two unpublished love poems, she invoked morning sounds, morning light. One begins:

> It is marvellous to wake up together
> At the same minute; marvellous to hear
> The rain begin suddenly all over the roof,
> To feel the air suddenly clear
> As if electricity had passed through it
> From a black mesh of wires in the sky.
> All over the roof the rain hisses,
> And below, the light falling of kisses.

This was written in the late 1930s or early 1940s. In 1974, in "Breakfast Song," however, the mornings had brought darker thoughts:

> My love, my saving grace,
> your eyes are awfully blue.

I kiss your funny face,
your coffee-flavored mouth.
Last night I slept with you.
Today I love you so
how can I bear to go
(as soon I must, I know)
to bed with ugly death

The business of standing back, of describing, of making statements, of attempting to depict things in nature with a detailed and forensic skill, belongs fundamentally to Bishop's time in Key West. She writes like someone in flight from something, in search of nourishment from seascapes and landscapes that were oddly provisional and might not last in the same way as people might not, indeed would not, last.

Yet history will not go away. In her notes for poems, she refers to Key West as Cayo Hueso, the Bone Key, reputed to be a Native American burial place. (Bishop considered using the title "Bone Key" for the volume that became *A Cold Spring*.) In her poem "Florida," she begins as though she is writing a breezy travel guide: "The state with the prettiest name." But quickly the mangrove roots "when dead strew white swamps with skeletons," and turtles "die and

leave their barnacled shells on the beaches, /
and their large white skulls with round eye-
sockets / twice the size of a man's." In the second stanza, there are buzzards "drifting down,
down, down," and slowly "the state with the
prettiest name" becomes "the careless, corrupt
state" and the alligator "speaks in the throat /
of the Indian Princess." While the poem suggests
human corruption and violence, it is nature
that does most of the damage in the poem, as
things rot and decay, as things fade and erode,
as if the battle, the real one, were going on in
the undergrowth, at the place where the land
meets the sea, or the place where things rot and
go back to some elemental state.

The people in the poems of Key West she saw
fit to publish are notable by their separateness
from her; they are fleeting presences, figures
glimpsed, and, as in all her work, there are many
absences. It is interesting that the figure most
vividly described is the fish that she let go in her
poem "The Fish," a poem that has both sweeter
and more savage echoes of a story from the life
of Jonathan Swift: "My greatest misery," Swift is
reported to have said, "is recollecting a scene of
twenty years past, and then all of a sudden drop-
ping into the present. I remember when I was a

little boy, I felt a great fish at the end of my line which I drew up almost on the ground, but it dropt in, and the disappointment vexeth me to this very day, and I believe it was the type of all my future disappointments."

In Bishop's unpublished poems from Key West, she wrote about the life she lived, the friends and lovers she had, but this did not satisfy her, or it could not be wielded into a completed poem; most of these unfinished Key West poems read like notes, scraps, words written down, too many words maybe, too much said, too much included.

In the unfinished ones about landscape, the landscape seems too easy with itself; in her finished poems about landscape and seascape, on the other hand, there is always some element—or in "Florida," many elements—that is disturbing or ambiguous, with its own pain, a pain she seems more comfortable noting than the actual pain she lived with, or kept at bay. In "Little Exercise," the palm trees are "suddenly revealed / as fistfuls of limp fish-skeletons." In "Seascape," the lighthouse is "skeletal." It is also in clerical dress, ready to warn ("He thinks that hell rages below his iron feet") that "heaven is not like this." Indeed, "Heaven is not like flying or swimming, /

but has something to do with blackness and a strong glare."

In "Cootchie," "the lighthouse will discover Cootchie's grave / and dismiss all as trivial; the sea, desperate, / will proffer wave after wave."

In many of these poems, written in a place that had been taken from the Native Americans, written in a time when war loomed or war was on, there are many images of war and battle. The roosters will fight each other,

> and one is flying,
> with raging heroism defying
> even the sensation of dying.

In "Little Exercise,"

> Now the storm goes away again in a series
> of small badly lit battle-scenes,
> each in "Another part of the field."

In "The Fish," five earlier hooks hanging from the fish's lips are first "weaponlike," then they seem like military honors:

> Like medals with their ribbons
> frayed and wavering,
> a fire-haired beard of wisdom
> trailing from his aching jaw.

In "Late Air," Bishop notes another set of five, the "five remote red lights" on "the Navy Yard aerial." (In the actual episode that inspired "The Fish," Bishop said, there were only three hooks, but for the poem, she made them into five. "I think it improved the poem when I made that change," she said.)

At the end of the poem "Florida," there is another image of five, this time the five "distinct calls" of the alligator: "friendliness, love, mating, war, and a warning." Even in "Songs for a Colored Singer," the war cannot be ignored:

Like an army in a dream
the faces seem,
darker, darker, like a dream.
They're too real to be a dream.

In "The Bight," even the birds are given an edge of violence. The pelicans crash into the water "unnecessarily hard, / it seems to me, like pickaxes," and

Black-and-white man-of-war birds soar
on impalpable drafts
and open their tails like scissors on the curves
or tense them like wishbones, till they
    tremble.

The house where Bishop lived in Key West has a lovely shadowy, provisional air. Like the house in Nova Scotia, it has elements of a toy clapboard house, something that could be easily dismantled. Great Village itself seemed to be built on borrowed land; so too during Bishop's time in Key West, all the houses were under threat from the military expansion. They were, in any case, nothing compared to the sea with all its persistent power. Her house in Key West was also close to the graveyard. Indeed, the graves themselves in Key West appeared more stable and permanent than the places where the living lived. The graves were there to stay; they knew their place. Just as birds in flight from the northern winter rest on the way, and find a place to stop and consider things and save their energy, Bishop's time in Key West seems like a glorious preparation for a journey further away from the North, further toward the healing light of the South.

The Escape from History

In September 1952 Elizabeth Bishop wrote from Brazil to her doctor in New York: "I still feel I must have died and gone to heaven." And in April 1953 she wrote to a friend: "This place is wonderful. . . . I only hope you don't have to get to be forty-two before you feel so at home."

She began to send letters about her daily life in Brazil to friends: "I looked out of the window at seven this morning and saw my hostess in a bathrobe directing the blowing up of a huge boulder with dynamite." She learned to drive, and she and Lota de Macedo Soares, who was her hostess and her lover, owned a good number of fancy sports cars. She described Lota mending a puncture: "She had on a wrap-around skirt which had fallen open as she bent over & and there was a little white behind, dressed in really old-fashioned long white drawers, exposed to the oncoming truck drivers."

Domestic life at the modern house Lota built in Petrópolis outside Rio became a subject for great amusement, as though it was a play Bishop was acting in, a comedy she had invented, something not quite serious, a parody of "normal" life. They kept servants and lots of domestic

pets and a cook who was, according to one letter, "half-savage and very dirty." Then, "while
we were away, the cook took up painting—
proving that art only flourishes in leisure time,
I guess. . . . Hers are getting better and better,
and the rivalry between us is intense—if I paint
a picture she paints a bigger and better one; if
I cook something she immediately cooks the
same thing only using all the eggs. I don't think
she knows about poetry yet, but probably that
will come."

But she followed that last description (in a
letter to Robert Lowell) with an observation that
anyone who comes from a northern landscape
will recognize: "But oh dear—my aunt writes
me long descriptions of the 'fall colors' in Nova
Scotia and I wonder if that's where I shouldn't be
after all." In almost all of the letters there was a
sense that her own fragility and instability had
made her respond to Brazil with such openness
and gusto. In nearly all of them there was an almost desperate urge, despite her regrets, to remain cheerful.

While the displacements of the distant past
and the rumble of war animated the imagery of
the poems written in Florida, once Bishop began
to live in Brazil, she was interested in escaping

history, or evoking it only as a way of allowing it to fade, dissolve, or forming an ironic, almost amused response to it, minimizing its power and force as she had done in the opening part of her early poem "Over 2,000 Illustrations and a Complete Concordance," in which she wrote of the engraving of "the squatting Arab, / or groups of Arabs, plotting, probably, / against our Christian Empire."

Some of her Brazil poems offer statements arising merely from close observation; there is much luscious description. "Arrival at Santos," her first, begins as does "The Map" with the idea that nothing much could be said, and that every statement would thus have to seem simple, or chiseled from other statements: "Here is a coast; here is a harbor." And then there was, she wrote, "some scenery." The mountains may be "self-pitying," but "who knows?" And the palms maybe be "tall," but they are also "uncertain." When she sees the flag of Brazil, she "somehow never thought of there *being* a flag." And she presumes then, as she embarks, that there will be coins and paper money. She hopes that "the customs officials will speak English." At the end of the poem, when she says "we are driving to the interior," this is simply what she means. It is the interior of a new country. It is not the interior of herself. She wishes to look outward; that is why she has come here.

In her love poem "The Shampoo," written to Lota, Time, the thing that once reached his hand in "and tumbled us out," has suddenly become benign. "For Time is," she writes now, "nothing if not amenable."

There is something strange, almost coy and whimsical and naïve, about her idea that Brazil would not have a flag or that Time there would be "nothing if not amenable." At the beginning of the next poem she makes a statement that is questionable but, in the light of her need to escape, to wriggle free for as long as she can, from places haunted by history or by personal memory, almost understandable. The poem is called "Brazil, January 1, 1502," and it marks the date when Portuguese explorers sailed into a bay they mistook for the mouth of a river and called the place "Rio de Janeiro," after their month of arrival. "Nature," she says at the opening of the poem, "greets our eyes / exactly as she must have greeted theirs."

How strange that she would have allowed such a thought to linger, or be written down! Surely she must have meant "almost exactly"? After all, she wrote at the end of "At the Fishhouses" that "our knowledge is historical." In the euphoria of those early days away from North America, much of her writing made Brazilians seem less than real and Brazil itself a tapestry or a fairy tale, or a play, or even a pantomime, created for her pleasure. Even the colonial drama seems less than real. The arriving Christians are "hard as nails" but also "tiny as nails," and in this "tapestried landscape," the violence enacted is a distant, childlike game, or an ironic tapestry, as the Christians were "each out to catch an Indian for himself" and the Indians' "maddening little women . . . kept calling, / calling to each other (or had the birds waked up?) / and retreating, always retreating, behind it."

Bishop wanted a Brazil not only free of memories, a place where our knowledge was not historical, but also a place de-politicized. Since for her and for Lota, because of their associates and their politics, it would not always be so, then we must allow her this early freedom to exoticize the country where rain will remind her, in "Questions of Travel," of

> politicians' speeches:
> two hours of unrelenting oratory
> and then a sudden golden silence.

In search of the "sudden golden silence," she would begin by writing poems about people she saw, people she barely understood, as in Key West she wrote about Jerónimo's house and Cootchie and, in prose, the primitive painter Gregorio Valdes.

In Key West, underlying the poems about landscape and seascape was the notion of death and the idea of violence. Once Bishop moved to Brazil, these images tend to disappear. She was a poet whose physical surroundings entered her spirit. Thus in the early poems that deal with Brazil, there is a new emphasis on landscape and description, and a new sort of imagery emerges that takes its bearings from property and rights. In "Squatter's Children," for example, the girl and boy are "specklike" and near "a specklike house." The children stand "among / the mansions you may choose / out of a bigger house than yours." This bigger house may be the world, or the wider society. In any case, its "lawfulness endures. / Its soggy documents retain / your rights in rooms of falling rain."

In "Manuelzinho," the object of the poem is a wayward servant, "Half squatter, half tenant (no rent)—/ a sort of inheritance"; the poem is a whimsical exercise in exasperation at the servant's shortcomings and eccentricities. In "The Burglar of Babylon," written in ballad form, the poverty of Rio is described as though the people are birds:

> On the hills a million people,
> A million sparrows, nest,
> Like a confused migration
> That's had to light and rest,
>
> Building its nests, or houses,
> Out of nothing at all, or air.

While most of Bishop's Brazilian poems are exploratory or whimsical or exquisitely created and awestruck, there are two poems that stand alone, two poems that have a frightened, shivering quality and combine a steeliness of observation with careful, close attention. These poems are distilled and then suggestive, Bishop at her most rigorous. The earlier of the two, "The Armadillo," uses a diction filled with coiled simplicity; there is a tight meter and a scheme that allows many words of one syllable ("night/height"; "parts/hearts"; "stars/Mars"; "toss/Cross") to rhyme.

The poem opens with a customary casualness as she describes a scene that she might have happened on a few times, a scene in which "frail, illegal fire balloons" appear in the sky over Rio. As in "The Moose," she trails long sentences through several stanzas, playing a conversational slackness against an elaborate system of syntactical and metrical control. The tone is distant, precise, and almost amused. There are some signals, however, of an undertone. There is something almost ominous about the idea that "the paper chambers" fill with a light that comes and goes "like hearts." In the fifth stanza, as the balloons are "steadily forsaking us," Bishop allows for the first time a rhyme that is not pure, rhyming "forsaking us" with "dangerous."

Gradually, then, the balloons, which seem merely pretty and can be described with relish as they wander in the sky, become lethal, as one of them lands on an owls' nest and burns it and displaces the owls and then a baby rabbit and an armadillo. Then in the very last stanza, which is in italics, Bishop takes an enormous risk. The casual and descriptive tone becomes sharp, stark, alarming:

> *Too pretty, dreamlike mimicry!*
> *O falling fire and piercing cry*
> *and panic, and a weak mailed fist*
> *clenched ignorant against the sky!*

Her knowledge here is not only historical, it is more immediate than it has ever been before, filled not only with knowledge but with current fear and pressing alarm. It is not the past that disturbs Bishop, but the present. She has let the present into a poem. The word "ignorant" in the last line makes us think of the ending of Matthew Arnold's "Dover Beach":

Ah, love, let us be true
To one another! for the world, which seems
To lie before us like a land of dreams,
So various, so beautiful, so new
Hath really neither joy, nor love, nor light,
Nor certitude, nor peace, nor help for pain,
And we are here as on a darkling plain
Swept with confused alarms of struggle and
    flight,
Where ignorant armies clash by night.

"The Armadillo" tempers the other Brazilian poems; it erases the whimsy, the urge merely to describe. The scene may be exotic at its opening and filled with new delight; by the end there has been mayhem, dislocation, cruelty, powerlessness. The poem, in its way, enacts what happened to Bishop in Brazil. Her time there began with happiness and newfound love. Slowly, as Lota took on a more public role in society and allied herself with a number of politicians, the relationship between her and Bishop grew fraught.

Bishop's letters to Robert Lowell and others throw interesting light on her years in Brazil. Some of the letters are comic masterpieces about the antics of the weather, the servants, the locals, and various pets. But a number of letters emphasize the role of Lota de Macedo Soares in the political life of Brazil and the sort of alliances and allegiances she had, some of which became dark and nasty. They emphasize too the idea that Bishop, when she thought about politics in Brazil, was both passionately engaged and hopelessly out of her depth.

Lota's alliances centered on the figure of Carlos Lacerda, a conservative Brazilian politician and staunch anti-Communist. Lacerda survived an assassination attempt in 1954, two years after Bishop's arrival in Brazil. This attempt was organized by the president of Brazil, who committed suicide as a result of its failure. Bishop wrote an unpublished poem about the event called "Suicide of a Moderate Dictator," which is dedicated to Carlos Lacerda. In 1955 Bishop wrote to Lowell: "A friend and neighbor of mine, Carlos Lacerda (if you ever read any news items about

Brazil you must have heard of him in the past year—the young man who was really responsible for the fall and suicide of president Vargas) is flying up to New York in a few days, and I'm giving him a small present to be mailed to you."

Later, in 1955, after an attempted coup in Brazil had failed, she wrote to Lowell again: "One of my best friends here was the leader of the revolution that didn't come off. . . . He's a wonderful man really . . . and may end up as anything, of course, even dictator; Catholic, but liberally so. Well—he had to flee the country." In 1959 she wrote again about Lacerda as being "such a good example of the power-type—of which most poets are (or of which I am) so ignorant. . . . If the next elections go the way it looks as if they might, Carlos may get to be vice-president (even president, eventually) or at least Minister of Education."

In 1961 Lacerda became governor of the state of Guanabara, which included the city of Rio de Janeiro. Bishop wrote to Lowell: "Lota was invited by Carlos Lacerda to work for him and we both feel it is very important for her. . . . He has put Lota in charge of a huge new 'fill' along the Rio bay . . . and enough land besides to build restaurants, parks, playgrounds, outdoor cafés. . . . Lota has just about the world's best landscape gardener working with her, and four of the best architects here—and Rio being the way it is, of course they're all old friends and it is all fine so far."

In 1963 she wrote to say that Carlos was going to run for president in 1965, and if he won "I'm sure Lota would be Minister of Education or an Ambassador or something. . . . I think she is really the only friend he has." Later that year, she described an episode in which Carlos had arrived at the country house that Bishop shared with Lota: "All lights [were] on in our house and strange men on the terrace . . . then who should appear but Carlos—all were armed. . . . We think—but don't know—he started off for his own house and was probably followed, or found his house surrounded, or something. There was an attempt to kidnap him last week, too."

In April 1964, when Lacerda was barricaded inside the governor's palace, Lota was with him. "She had a safe-conduct from one of the generals," Bishop wrote. "April 1, Carlos broadcast an appeal for *help*, sounding really desperate. I got it in short wave. . . . That was the worst moment—I knew Lota was inside—she'd insisted on going back—or hoped she was, and not picked up by the Federal army. However—an hour later it was all over." Carlos and Lota had survived. "Now for two days they've been putting people in prison—oh God—most of the big shots got away. . . . Over 3,000 prisoners taken in Rio alone. Carlos has issued orders over and over, no police brutality to be allowed, etc.—but incidents will happen with any police."

In a letter written a few days after these events, Bishop wrote to Lowell: "But this *isn't* my world—or is it?" On the next day, however, she wrote defending Lacerda and vehemently attacking the negative coverage of him in the United States press, which had argued "that it's wrong to take away civil rights. Well—ideally speaking, of course—but what do you do in a weak, poor country, without any police at all, to speak of?" Toward the end of the letter, she wrote: "Forgive me—I *won't* say anymore, but confine myself to Wordsworthian notes from now on." The following year she wrote about Brazilian politics: "I CAN'T understand the situation. . . . Everything seems worse, that's all."

Things also began to deteriorate in the relationship between Bishop and Lota. Once Carlos Lacerda had ceased to be governor, Lota came under a great deal of pressure as she attempted, despite opposition, to continue her work on creating the park in Rio; Bishop was drinking and spending time in the town of Ouro Preto, away from Rio. At the end of 1965, Bishop went to teach in Seattle, where she had an affair with a younger woman. Things were no better when she returned, as Lota suffered a nervous breakdown. One of their friends remembered: "When Lota began to be sick, Elizabeth began to be unhappy. . . . The government had changed. The new governor wasn't doing what Lota had hoped he would do for her in the park . . . and Lota would cry a lot." By the end of November 1966, Lota "was in hospital," according to Brett C. Millier in *Elizabeth Bishop: Life and the Memory of It*, and "heavily medicated and sleeping many hours a day. Elizabeth, unable to stand the strain or be alone while Lota was away, went off to Ouro Preto. . . . Elizabeth talked to Lota twice a day on the phone, she said, but stayed away ten days longer than she had intended, unwilling to return and face the barrage of criticism and the guilt it inspired."

Lota de Macedo Soares committed suicide while in New York with Bishop in 1967. Bishop wrote to friends: "Lota died Monday morning sometime without having regained consciousness. . . . She was a wonderful, remarkable woman. . . . I had the 12 or 13 happiest years of my life with her, before she got sick—and I suppose that is a great deal in this unmerciful world." To other friends, she wrote: "I am just trying not to blame myself for all the wrong things I know I did. She was a wonderful, remarkable woman—and no one will ever know what really happened." To another friend: "I don't think she had consciously planned this because she so brought so many things—12 kilo bags of coffee, etc. We were together a few hours, really. She was exhausted, and sick, and very depressed. I think perhaps she felt some miracle would take place and she'd feel better the minute she got to New York. I'll never really know—and of course can't help blaming myself. I tried to cheer her up . . . but still feel I must have let her down badly somehow or other. *We had no quarrel*—everything was peaceful and affectionate—honestly; you MUST believe that— went to bed early, and of course I feel if only I hadn't been so tired and slept so hard I might have saved her."

In 1968 Bishop moved to San Francisco but continued to spend some time in Brazil. In 1970 she taught Lowell's class at Harvard and met Alice Methfessel there; they became partners. In 1973 Bishop bought an apartment at Lewis Wharf in Boston, where once more she had a view of the ocean, as she had had in Rio.

If her first great poem about Brazil is "The Armadillo," written in 1957, the second, "Santarém," was written twenty-one years later, the year before she died. It is infused, like her best work about Nova Scotia, with a sense of loss, a feeling that she is describing a scene with the helpless tone of a lone survivor trying to make sense of whatever has occurred, or whatever is in front of her eyes. Once more, she begins casually, in a tone almost distracted, as though she were in mid-sentence: "Of course I may be remembering it all wrong / after, after—how many years?"

And then it begins, the memory of a place at the conflux of two rivers—the Tapajós and the Amazon. The poem puzzles over ideas of dualities and opposites (as does the last line of "Roosters": "faithful as enemy, or friend"). Lota has been dead more than a decade now, and the letters Bishop wrote to her have been destroyed by Lota's friends. This is one reason she might be remembering the scene "all wrong," since she had planned to use those letters as a source. In any case, she seems to be alone as she contemplates the scene, what she describes in one of her most beautiful phrases as "that watery, dazzling dialectic."

The voice is stable; the whimsy remains at the edge of things, tempered by the old gravity. Bishop still loves describing things—"lots of mongrel / riverboats" and "a sky of gorgeous, under-lit clouds." She is almost ready to create a comfortable and cozy scene, made for tourists, with "everything bright, cheerful, casual—or so it looked." That "or so it looked" offers a signature cautionary moment, almost like a moment in the chamber music of Anton Webern, which Bishop listened to a great deal in Brazil, when there is a way of not giving into the melody, of holding it back, diverting it, hinting at it sweetly, and then allowing a jarring note to enter and be entertained.

As the poem proceeds, the poet watches the crowds and the mild chaos with amusement and detachment. And then in the last stanza, "in the blue pharmacy," she sees an empty wasps' nest. Years before, in a poem from Key West called "Jerónimo's House," she had compared the house itself and all its detail and beauty to a wasps' nest:

My house, my fairy
　　palace, is
of perishable
　　clapboards with
three rooms in all,
　　my gray wasps' nest
of chewed-up paper
　　glued with spit.

In the poem, that house is a haven, filled with
images of comfort and odd happiness; "my shel-
ter from / the hurricane," which was all Bishop
sought as she moved south. In "Santarém," once
more, the image returns. It is "small, exquisite,
clean matte white, / and hard as stucco."

The pharmacist gives her the wasps' nest as a
gift. Back on board, a fellow tourist, who is "the
retiring head of Philips Electric," asks: "What is
that ugly thing?" His question has the last word in
the poem, but it is clear somehow that the answer
will prevail, and that the answer is contained in
the perfection of the nest which the wasps made
for themselves, which has survived, just as "blue
eyes, English names, / and *oars*" have survived
history in this part of the Amazon. The answer
is also contained in the sense of ease, calmness,
and completion in this landscape, as though

nature and culture, despite the thunderstorms and the marks of history, had come to some understanding.

It is enough now that the nest has been re-membered and can be invoked. It is the closest to a symbolic object in Bishop's entire work; it will also remind her of a home that was once complete. But, by its presence in the poem as a real and single object, something seen and re-membered and carefully described, it will resist any effort to make it more than it appears.

Grief and Reason

In the month or so after Thom Gunn died in April 2004, I formed the habit at the end of my own day's work of going into the back room of my house in Dublin, the room with the books, and taking down his *Collected Poems* and reading a poem.

I remember thinking on one of those nights that the poems which seemed most powerful to me were the ones that dealt with solitude, and that there was a sort of loneliness in all of Gunn's diction, which could easily be misunderstood as just spareness or plainness.

One night I noticed a small book beside the *Collected Poems* called *Thom Gunn in Conversation with James Campbell*. I took it down and, casually, not having read it before, began to read it. On page 19 I came on the following passage that made me sit up for a moment. Campbell asked, "Your new book, *Boss Cupid*, contains some new poems about your mother. Is this the first time you've written about her?" Gunn, in his reply, mentioned a short poem also in the new book called "My Mother's Pride" (which ended with the line "I am made by her, and undone") and went on:

The second poem about my mother is called "The Gas Poker." She killed herself, and my brother and I found the body, which was not her fault because she'd barred the doors, as you'll see in the poem. Obviously this was quite a traumatic experience; it would be in anyone's life. I wasn't able to write about it till just a few years ago. Finally I found the way to do it was really obvious: to withdraw the first person, and to write about it in the third person. Then it became easy, because it was no longer about myself.

I looked at the words again: "Obviously this was quite a traumatic experience; it would be in anyone's life." And then I crossed the room and burrowed among some books and found the quote I was looking for. It was in David Kalstone's *Becoming a Poet*, and it was from a letter that Elizabeth Bishop wrote to Anne Stevenson in 1964: "Although I think I have a prize 'unhappy childhood,' almost good enough for the text-books—please don't think I dote on it." In that letter, Bishop wrote about her mother's mental illness. "One always thinks that things might be better now, she might have been cured, etc. . . . Well—there we are. Times have changed. I have several friends who are, have been, will be etc. insane; they discuss it all very freely and I've visited asylums many times since. But in 1916 things were different. After a couple of years, unless you cured yourself, all hope was abandoned—"

"Well—there we are." I looked at the words again and put them beside Gunn's: "Obviously this was quite a traumatic experience. It would be in anyone's life." And then I put "please don't think I dote on it" beside "to withdraw the first person, and write about it in the third person." And then I found another book, by the Russian poet Joseph Brodsky, whose title essay, "On Grief and Reason," dealt in some detail with Robert Frost's poem "Home Burial." "So what was it that he was after in this, his very own poem?" Brodsky wrote. "He was, I think, after grief and reason, which, while poison to each other, are language's most efficient fuel—or, if you will, poetry's indelible ink."

And now I had come across it in Bishop and Gunn, grief masked by reason, grief and reason battling it out.

I did not need to look for the introduction to my own book *Love in a Dark Time*, written some years earlier, in which I had named Thom Gunn, Elizabeth Bishop, Thomas Mann, and James Baldwin as four writers I was reading in my late teens with considerable intensity without knowing that they were gay. *Love in a Dark Time* had essays on all four, written then as a way to recover these writers, relate to them, almost get in touch with them as a gay writer myself. And now, this night, in this room, with these books on the table—Gunn's *Collected Poems*, James Campbell's interview with Gunn, David Kalstone's book on Elizabeth Bishop and her friends, and Joseph Brodsky's *On Grief and Reason*, I realized that I had maybe been mistaken when I thought that the reason the poems of Gunn and Bishop and the fiction of Baldwin and Mann had hit me emotionally with exceptional force was because the authors were gay.

Homosexuality was only part of the story. The other part of the story was that each of the four writers had lost a parent in childhood or early adulthood. Whereas Mann and Baldwin had dealt with this directly, or at least ironically or polemically—in Mann's early novel *Buddenbrooks*, for example, or in Baldwin's *Notes of a Native Son*—Bishop and Gunn, in a confessional age, had masked their grief with reason. The tone of impersonality, of passive description, of an immense and powerful withholding, lay at the core of their work, and it was something I recognized.

In a *Paris Review* interview, done in the early 1990s, Gunn distinguished between two different strengths that can be summoned in the writing of poetry, one he called "a very conscious arranging strength, keeping things in schematic form," and the other "the stuff you can call primitive or unconscious."

Both Elizabeth Bishop and Thom Gunn set about keeping themselves distant from the reader. They described the world as though they watched it rather than fully took part in it; they used a tone of neutrality and separateness; they made clear that they were not writing to seek help from the reader or look for spiritual nourishment by exploring themselves or their feelings in the poem. Rather, Bishop wrote from a position of uneasy, deep-seated fastidiousness and wonder at even the smallest object, and Gunn enjoyed having power and control over meter and rhythm and line; he displayed a deep interest in judgment, will, strength, and brute force.

Both poets made a point of living in and describing the ordinary universe and observing its citizens; they wrote poems about the slightest things. Their poems move constantly between tones and textures that loosen and tighten and loosen again, which speak clearly and then hush and quieten more.

Faced with thoughts and things, they sought to rectify, justify, or at times evade by firm control and clear, precise description. It was as though they had just arrived in the world and were almost pleased and then somewhat puzzled by its strategies and began soon to invent their own. Gunn wrote about the poet Gary Snyder: "Like most serious poets he is concerned at finding himself on a barely known planet, in an almost unknown universe, where he must attempt to create and discover meanings." When James Campbell asked Gunn, at the end of their interview, if this could be Thom Gunn describing Thom Gunn, Gunn replied: "I expect so." It could also be Elizabeth Bishop.

Unlike Gary Snyder, however, both Gunn and Bishop were capable of immensely formal but oddly plain poetic diction; they often created elaborate formal structures in their poems; they exuded elegance and, at times in the case of Gunn, what Frank Kermode called "a chaste tone." And they wrote endings to poems that sometimes seemed to hover between conclusion and uncertainty, between what became known as closure and a sense that there was too much regret between the words for closure ever to be possible.

In the work of both Bishop and Gunn, words meant simply what they said, and thus had to be chosen and weighed with immense precision and dark care. Their poems took their bearings from what Gunn wrote about Ben Jonson: "the coolness, the formality, the eschewing of any striking rhetorical techniques, the general sense of external occasion dominating the poem." Words for Gunn and Bishop meant business and did not give change. When the critic David Kalstone read Bishop's "In the Waiting Room" and came across the lines: "Suddenly, from inside, / came an *oh!* of pain," he understood the word "inside" as possibly ambiguous, as obviously meaning inside the dentist's room but also maybe inside the little girl's head, "a moment of involuntary identification." Bishop, when she read his interpretation of the poem, was so disturbed at his misreading of the word "inside," which she had meant in only one concrete and precise way—to signify inside the dentist's office as opposed to outside in the waiting room— that she phoned Kalstone long-distance to say "that 'inside' did *not* have a multiple reference and that perhaps rather than mislead readers she should change the line."

Both Gunn and Bishop were capable of elegant whimsy as well as clear, reasonable poetic diction; they made playful games with poetic form in poems like Gunn's early poem "Round and Round":

> The lighthouse keeper's world is round,
> Belongings skipping in a ring —
> All that a man may want therein,
> A wife, a wireless, bread, jam, soap,
> Yet day by night his straining hope
> Shoots out to live upon the sound
> The spinning waves make while they break
> For their own endeavour's sake—
> The lighthouse keeper's world is round.

Bishop, as we have seen, also wrote about lighthouses, and her tone could also in some of the poems be playful, almost light, as in "Cirque d'Hiver":

> She stands upon her toes and turns and turns.
> A slanting spray of artificial roses
> is stitched across her skirt and tinsel bodice.
> Above her head she poses
> another spray of artificial roses.

Both she and Gunn also wrote strange, almost surreal poems about figures half-human, half-animal, or animals that had qualities entirely human, or humans who were secretly animals, poems such as Bishop's "The Man-Moth" or Gunn's "The Allegory of the Wolf Boy" or "Moly," the title poem of his 1971 collection. They both were opposed to attitudes in poetry that seemed high-flown and untested by the detail of casual experience. For example, they both, without consulting each other, wrote parodies of Stephen Spender's poem "I think continually of those who were truly great." Gunn's began:

> I think of all the toughs through history
> And thank heaven that they lived,
> > continually,
> I praise the overdogs from Alexander
> To those who would not play with Stephen
> > Spender.

In a letter to Randall Jarrell written in February 1965, Bishop confessed that she had written a poem called "I practically never think of those who were truly great" but added that she had never dared to print it.

Both Gunn and Bishop, having been brought up partly by aunts, partly in houses where they did not feel at home, left where they were from and settled in beautiful and exotic cities on the ocean with hills. Bishop went to Rio, and Gunn left England in 1954, at the age of twenty-four, and lived most of his life in San Francisco. They both wrote about these cities and their inhabitants with relish, relief, wonder; they became great noticers. While there are moments in letters and poems when Bishop makes clear that she sometimes missed Nova Scotia, where her mother came from and where she spent her early childhood, Gunn, despite the stray references to memories of England in his work, was careful never to miss home. "I don't know why I left England," he told James Campbell. "I don't know why I'm so happy not living there."

In many of the statements Gunn and Bishop made in their poems, there is a great reticence. It was the reticence that hit me when I first read their poems, and still hits me, with considerable emotional force. I found something in the space between the words, in the hovering between tones at the end of stanzas, at the end of poems themselves, in the elegance, in the watchfulness and use of the solitary figure either speaking or being described, which made me sit up and realize that something important was being hidden and something equally important was being said.

Both poets had a way of handling catastrophe as though it were nothing, or nothing much. Gunn wrote a calm poem, "No Speech from the Scaffold," that begins:

> There will be no speech from
> the scaffold, the scene must
> be its own commentary.

Just as Bishop in "Little Exercise" insisted that we imagine the figure who has been through the storm as "sleeping in the bottom of a row-boat / tied to a mangrove root or the pile of a bridge; / think of him as uninjured, barely disturbed," so, too, for both of them, death barely disturbs. Gunn, in "Elegy," the first poem in *The Passages of Joy* (1982), consoles himself with:

> Even the terror
> of leaving life like that
> better than the terror
> of being unable to handle it.

And Bishop, in "First Death in Nova Scotia," manages to maintain an exquisite, childlike distance from the death of her cousin in childhood: "Arthur's coffin was / a little frosted cake," and

"Arthur was very small. / He was all white, like a doll / that hadn't been painted yet."

Halfway through his career—in the mid-1970s—Gunn came out in his poetry and wrote explicitly about his homosexuality. When she died, Elizabeth Bishop left poems, and sometimes fragments of poems, that dramatized or dealt directly with her lesbianism, but she published only coded lesbian poems. She did not publish the uncoded poems in her lifetime; most of the time, she left her sexuality out of her work. Bishop, in an interview, wondered: "Can one ever have *enough* defenses?" She believed, she said, "in closets, closets and more closets."

Both Gunn and Bishop had great reservations about what was called "confessional poetry," which became fashionable in the 1960s. "The tendency is to overdo the morbidity. You just wished they kept some of these things to themselves," Bishop said. Gunn told James Campbell: "I don't like dramatizing myself. I don't want to be Sylvia Plath. The last person I want to be!" Later in the interview he said: "I'm not interested in confessional poetry." On the subject of self-pity, Gunn told Campbell: "I suppose it's a bad thing morally to give way to.

People who are sorry for themselves are boring, aren't they?" In a letter to Robert Lowell, Bishop wrote: "Sometimes I wish we could have a more sensible conversation about this suffering business, anyway. I imagine we agree fairly well—it is just that I guess I think it is so inevitable & unavoidable there's no use talking about it, & then in itself it has no value anyway." Later in the same letter she added: "I like this story from the N.Y. Times—a composition by a child in the 3rd grade: 'I told my little brother that when you die you cannot breathe and he did not say a word. He just kept on playing.'"

It was easy to feel that what she and Thom Gunn learned to leave out of their texts, the way, like the little brother in the *New York Times*, they did not say a word and kept on playing, made all the difference to their tone. Mary McCarthy, who knew Bishop when they were both students at Vassar (and who, Bishop believed, based the character of Lakey on her in McCarthy's novel *The Group*), said of her: "I envy the mind hiding in her words, like an 'I' counting up to a hundred waiting to be found." James Merrill wrote of Bishop's "instinctive, modest, lifelong impersonations of an ordinary woman." In his *Paris Review* interview, Thom Gunn agreed that "strategies of evasion . . . may contribute to what makes a poem successful."

Both Bishop and Gunn made clear in interviews—and, indeed, in the poems they wrote—their debt to poets of the sixteenth and seventeenth centuries rather than, say, Romantic poets or modernist poets. Bishop expressed her admiration for George Herbert's "absolute naturalness of tone," saying that he had been "the most important and lasting influence on me." In interviews she mentioned what Coleridge had said about Herbert, "that he wrote about the most fantastic things imaginable in perfectly simple everyday language. That is what I have always tried to do."

While Bishop did not write a single finished poem about her mother's breakdown and incarceration, she wrote the story "In the Village" soon after her arrival in Brazil in 1952. This story dealt with her mother's breakdown and her own witnessing of what happened; later, she said that she produced it in two nights under the influence of a "combination of cortisone and the gin and tonic I had in the middle of the night." It was published in the *New Yorker* in December 1953— she bought a secondhand MG with the money.

"In the Village" was, Bishop wrote to a friend, "completely autobiographical." Ten years later she wrote to another friend: "'In the Village' is *entirely* not partly autobiographical. I've just compressed the time a little and perhaps put two summers together, or put things a bit out of sequence—but it's all straight fact." When Lowell read "In the Village" first, he wrote to Bishop wondering how autobiographical it was. Afterward, he wrote to her that it read "as though you weren't writing at all, but just talking in a full noisy room, talking until suddenly everyone is quiet."

When Lowell published his poem "The Scream" in *For the Union Dead*, he acknowledged that it was based on Bishop's story. He wrote to her with news that he had made a poem from her story: "I tried versing your 'In the Village' . . . your prose put into three-beat lines and probably a travesty, making something small and literary out [of] something much larger, gayer and more healthy. I let the scream throw out the joyful *clang*. Anyway, I send it with misgivings. Maybe you could use it for raw material for a really great poem."

When she read the poem that Lowell had made from her story, Bishop wrote to him: "'The

Scream' really works well, doesn't it. The story is far enough behind me so I can see it as a poem now. The first few stanzas I saw only my story— then the poem took over—and the last stanza is wonderful. It builds up beautifully, and everything of importance is there. But I was very surprised."

It is obvious why she was surprised, but perhaps she should not have been. The difference between "In the Village" and "The Scream" is the difference between two sensibilities. Bishop's "beautiful, calm story," as Lowell put it in his acknowledgments, was filled with mystery, nothing was overexplained or overemphasized. It would be easy to miss the point of the story. The pain was in the tone. The scream was all the more powerful because it was almost, but not quite, shrugged off as nothing. It was barely dramatized, the references to what happened, to the circumstances that effectively left Bishop an orphan, managed in the story obliquely, indirectly, and, of course, in prose, a medium that was not Bishop's natural medium.

The story opens:

A scream, the echo of a scream, hangs over that Nova Scotia village. No one hears it; it

hangs there forever, a slight stain in those
pure blue skies, skies that travellers compare
to those of Switzerland, too dark, too blue, so
that they seem to keep on darkening a little
more around the horizon—or is it around the
rims of the eyes?—the color of cloud or bloom
on the elm trees, the violet on the fields of
oats; something darkening over the woods
and waters as well as the sky. The scream
hangs like that, unheard, in memory—in the
past, in the present, and those years between.
It was not even loud to begin with, perhaps.
It just came there to live, forever—not loud,
just alive, forever. Its pitch would be the pitch
of my village. Flick the lightning rod on top
of the church steeple with your fingernail and
you will hear it.

In a letter to Robert Lowell in 1955, Bishop
tried to work out what the difference between
prose and poetry might be for her, which might
have caused her to derive "a great satisfaction"
from the few stories she wrote, including "In
the Village." "It's almost impossible not to tell
the truth in poetry, I think," she wrote, "but in
prose it keeps eluding one in the funniest way."
For most of her life, Bishop was interested in

managing what eluded her with considerable care so that the truth, when it appeared, might become sharper and more precise, the more she could find the right tone and form for it.

Lowell allowed the scream in Bishop's story to become a shriek in his poem. While he may have done this rather brilliantly, as she admitted, he was right to feel that Bishop, had she been ready, could have made "a really good poem" from this material. It was an essential aspect of her talent, indeed of her gift, as a poet, however, that she did not manage to confront what mattered to her most. Instead, she buried what mattered to her most in her tone, and it is this tone that lifts the best poems she wrote to a realm beyond their own occasion.

Bishop's efforts to break her silence about the facts of her upbringing did not just inspire Lowell to make a poem out of her story, but to write his own story in prose. His autobiographical piece "91 Revere Street" was written after he had read "In the Village" and included in his volume *Life Studies* (1959); it seemed, he wrote to Bishop, "thin and arty after your glorious mad mother and cow piece." Since he had followed her example, Bishop then in turn followed his, as though what they were doing was an intricate game of follow-the-leader, and thus included the story "In the Village" in her next volume of poetry, *Questions of Travel,* in 1965. Her editor, she wrote to Lowell, "at first said no, it was imitating you too much (it was)—but then when he'd read the story he changed his mind, and is now all for including it."

The Little That We Get for Free

It is not clear how much of Thom Gunn's work Bishop read. In her published correspondence, the first reference to him is in August 1968, when she was living in San Francisco and mentioned him in a letter to Robert Lowell: "Well, I've met some of the poets—and the only one I still really like is Thom Gunn." In October 1968 she wrote to Marianne Moore: "One poet I've met here, almost a neighbor, I like very much, Thom Gunn. His poetry is usually very good, I think; he's English but has lived here for a long time." The following year in February she did a reading with Gunn and other poets in a benefit for striking teachers at San Francisco State University and thought that "Gunn's poems and mine were the best," according to a letter she wrote to James Merrill. That April she wrote to another friend about the poets she had met in San Francisco: "But I like Thom Gunn best, I think."

Gunn remembered meeting Bishop for the first time in the spring of 1968: "I answered the phone one day and there was a very nice man I didn't know . . . who asked me to come and have drinks with him and Elizabeth Bishop because she wanted to meet me. Elizabeth had just moved to San Francisco. So I went over and there were Elizabeth and Suzanne [not the real name of her partner at that time], and Elizabeth was drunk out of her mind. We made polite conversation all evening while Elizabeth occasionally grunted out a monosyllable. The next day Suzanne phoned and wondered if I would like to try again. This time I was asked over to their place, and we got on wonderfully from then on.

"Elizabeth and I talked quite a lot during that year. . . . [I]t wasn't so that we spoke much about our private lives. That's what makes a real friendship, a close friendship. . . . She and I talked about poets we liked and specific poems that we liked and disliked. . . . I never let Elizabeth know this, but I didn't particularly like her poetry myself at that time. When I first got to know her, I took another look at her poetry. I wasn't greatly struck by it. There seemed to me something, for lack of a better word, that I'll call 'deeper' in her that hadn't gotten into the poetry. It wasn't until *Geography III*, with poems like "The Moose" that I saw that side of her. In a sense, with *Geography III* I can find more virtues in the earlier poetry than I could before. It reflects back on the earlier poetry."

In the *TLS* in 1990 Gunn set out to formulate how Bishop's last book of poems, *Geography III*, managed to change how he viewed her body of work. He described his early impression of her work as "coziness tinged with melancholy," displaying "dazzling powers all the more remarkable for their limitation." The poems in her first book, he wrote, were "like playthings, fresh-painted, decorative, charming, original, and yet tiny." He referred to the "inanity" of some of her poems. Then he wrote: "Her fifth book, *Geography III*, appeared in 1976, three years before her death, and here, all at once, everything was changed. Its longest three poems were directly concerned with uncontainable, unboxable experience. It was only ten poems long, and yet its achievement was such that it retrospectively altered the emphasis and shape of an entire career."

Geography III contained a prose poem and a translation and two quite slight short poems, filled with "coziness tinged with melancholy," as Gunn would have it. Thus there were really only six poems—"In the Waiting Room"; "Crusoe in England"; "The Moose"; "Poem"; "One Art"; and "The End of March"—and it was these six poems that changed Gunn's mind about Bishop's achievement.

In 1963 Robert Lowell had written to her that he "wished that slowing down to your pace might result in my rising a little nearer your standard." Lowell did not slow down his pace, and Bishop had slowed hers down further instead.

Each of the six poems written at this pace is a strange masterpiece, with a style that often seems relaxed until it becomes clear how much tension and calm pain are hidden in the diction, how much has been included and how much has been left out, and how deliberate the enterprise of making these poems has been.

All the drafts of the poem called "One Art," which ended as a villanelle, are reproduced in *Edgar Allan Poe & The Juke-Box*, the collection of Bishop's fragments and mostly unfinished poems published in 2006, edited by Alice Quinn. The poem began as a set of notes in prose with the title "The Art of Losing Things." It mentioned at first the loss or mislaying of small things such as reading-glasses and fountain pens and then went on to enumerate larger things lost such as "two whole houses" and "one peninsula and one island" and "a small-sized town," then "two whole cities . . . two of the world's biggest cities," then "one entire continent," and then, finally, the notes mentioned the loss of a person, a loved one.

These ideas slowly make their way into form, although much more quickly than most of Bishop's poems. "One Art" was written in a matter of months, whereas a poem like "The Moose" took, as we have seen, more than twenty-five years, which was, even for Bishop, a record. In January 1976 Bishop wrote to an editor at the *New Yorker:* "I am having a poem in your magazine fairly soon, I think—the one and only villanelle of my life. It is very SAD—it makes everyone weep, so I think it must be rather good, in its awful way, and I hope you will like it."

The last two stanzas of the poem read:

I lost two cities, lovely ones. And vaster,
some realms I owned, two rivers, a continent.
I miss them, but it wasn't a disaster.

—Even losing you (the joking voice, a gesture
I love) I shan't have lied. It's evident
the art of losing's not too hard to master
though it may look like (*Write* it!) like disaster.

In that last line, Bishop gave the impression that she was pushing herself as far as she could to state the terms of her predicament. What she was really doing, however, was playing a game between the deeply confessional and what remained ironic and withheld, refused, unmentionable, what she would not, in fact, write, despite her insistence, in the imperative, that she should. In all the things she lost that appeared in the final draft of the poem, from door keys to her mother's watch to houses, to the loved one, there was no mention of what she in her life had actually lost to start with—her father when she was eight months old and her mother when she was five, and then the home where she was brought up in Nova Scotia, from where she was removed by her father's family, and then Lota de Macedo Soares. There was also the villanelle form itself, with its rules and repetitions, a closed, playful form to contain experience rather than a way to release personal grief. As Eavan Boland has written: "In fact, the most disclosing statements of grief in Elizabeth Bishop's work are also the most ritualized. In 'Sestina' and in her celebrated villanelle 'One Art,' she entrusted some of her deepest intuitions of loss to two of the most complex game-forms in poetry."

Some of her friends, such as Frank Bidart and Octavio Paz, believed "One Art" to be "a confessional poem" and were surprised by it, but the critic Helen Vendler, who knew Bishop at Harvard toward the end of Bishop's life, saw something else in the poem. "There was some-thing very cold about Elizabeth," Vendler said. "You sensed her as a chilly person, not that she even perhaps wanted to be, but there was some residue of the person who could turn off. You felt that she could opt into privacy. . . . There is something about 'One Art' that reminds me of that part of her, where she says [in effect], 'I've lost it. I'm all by myself. Nobody's going to be able to take care of me. I'm not going to be able to hold on to anything. I am an encapsulated, isolated child.' Elizabeth had a place she could go in which she was all alone as a kind of frigid little girl. She could be enticed out of it, but then she would go back into it, back into her own aloneness."

While the poem may seem confessional, as it did to Bidart and Paz, and may seem personal, as it did to Vendler, there is a sense also in which the poem is almost playful, which is why it could be written so quickly and easily, "like writing a letter," as Bishop put it. "One Art" may indeed be read also as a poem about the fear of losing love; thus the list of things, flimsy and large, previously lost in the poem is merely a prepa-ration for the last loss. But it can also be read as a poem about what cannot be said, about losses too large to be mentioned, about what is between the lines of the poem rather than in the poem, about what Bishop has willfully, almost playfully, left out of the poem. Thus the losses enumerated are losses that cannot matter much, even if they look like disaster, because they can actually be mentioned.

What cannot be mentioned in the poem appeared four years afterward in a letter to Robert Lowell when Bishop was discussing how bad things were. In this letter, she suddenly moved, almost, it seems, without knowing, almost unwittingly, into creating the missing lines from her own poem "One Art" when she wrote for once, in private, what she could not bring herself to write in public, in an astonishing line with five beats like gasps or cries: "I lost my mother, and Lota, and others, too." These are the figures whom she survives; they are left out of the poetry.

This is not to suggest that the poem "One Art" was damaged by what was excluded, and not to suggest either that it would have been a better poem had she mentioned what she put in the letter. In that case, "One Art" would not have been a poem at all, because the tone of the poem depended on the tension between jokiness and self-pity, and on what was withheld, rather than on anything as banal as honesty. If honesty, full disclosure, were what was at stake, then the poem would not be one of the most memorable poems Bishop wrote, merely as ephemeral as a letter. Bishop, perhaps more than any other poet of her generation, especially more than Robert Lowell, knew the difference between a poem and a letter. Bishop spent her lifetime keeping the two apart for the benefit of the poem, with the exception perhaps of her poem "An Invitation to Miss Marianne Moore," which Thom Gunn, quite rightly, viewed as one of her most inane poems.

This business of Bishop's tone in her good poems is hard to define. Gunn wondered in 1990 how he could have overlooked "At the Fishhouses," which was published in her volume *A Cold Spring* in 1955. He wrote about "the gravity of the poem's conclusion, which treats of the sea both as alien and at the same time something we must try to relate to, like an important abstraction, 'like knowledge.'"

Twenty years after *A Cold Spring*, in *Geography III*, Bishop's cadences were milder, less grand and less rhapsodic, more subtle, but somehow also more insistent than "At the Fishhouses." In the poem entitled "Poem," for example, she describes a small painting given to her by a grand-uncle, a painting of a landscape in Nova Scotia with water meadow, cows, and geese. She wrote this poem in a voice that was almost her own voice, or in a voice that seemed so, of the scene depicted in the small painting.

This was Nova Scotia, the landscape of childhood, of her mother's family; it was the place where she had last seen her mother, the place she was taken away from by her father's family after her mother's incarceration. It became a place where holidays were spent, and then a place that she remembered. To call it home would be to miss the point. The place she recognized in the painting was a place of loss. Now might be the time—Bishop was in her sixties—to try finally in a poem to tell what happened.

It was not as though she did not try. Among her papers is a draft of a poem called "Homesickness" from the 1940s about her mother's early life as well as a story also called "Homesickness," which dealt with the same material. In a fragment from the early 1950s she asks: "Where are the dolls who loved me so / when I was young?" One of the names of the dolls is "Gertrude," her mother's name. And there is another draft of a poem from the 1970s, "And this was how it all began," that tried to deal with the poet's birth and her mother's madness, but it consisted of no more than stray phrases or scraps. So, too, from the 1970s she had notes for an elegy to Lota de Macedo Soares. "You are bored with us all. It is true we are boring. // the poor cats come for our breakfast / They hesitate at your door the Siamese gives a faint howl / they run and jump onto my bed // the smell of the earth, the smell of the black-roasted coffee / as fine as humus as black // no coffee can wake you no coffee can wake you no coffee can wake y // No coffee."

In these same years in her poem "Poem," Bishop was faced with the problem of what to do once she had recognized the precise place in the painting, what she called "this literal small backwater" that she had known as well as the painter. Her vision, as she says, had coincided with that of her grand-uncle the painter, but then she wondered in the poem if "vision" was the right word and concluded no, "vision is too serious a word." Instead, it would be "our looks, two looks." She was in search of more modest terms to describe a set of feelings that were dark and complex and must be rendered faithfully.

Now, she moved very slowly, as she sought to end the poem. Nothing would be said but everything suggested. The tone would be filled with helpless reverie, infinite and puzzled regret. Nothing would be stated too clearly, no names, no scenes recalled, no direct mention, for example, of how she might feel. Instead, in the poem, she looked at the painting again and remembered the scene and looked at what she remembered:

> Life and the memory of it cramped,
> dim, on a piece of Bristol board,
> dim, but how live, how touching in detail

And then a slow recognition that this was a place of loss, but that to name the loss would be to lose it further, to lose what was remembered and what was experienced, to betray it somehow. Instead, she would revert to the melancholy to which Gunn referred, but this time with no possible coziness:

> —the little that we get for free,
> the little of our earthly trust. Not much.
> About the size of our abidance
> along with theirs

"Not much." These two words would withstand that test which she had formulated in the letter to Lowell. "It's impossible not to tell the truth in poetry." And then, once those two words, so calm, calculated, scrupulous, and not to be contradicted, had been uttered, there was nothing more to be said, or almost nothing; it was essential, Bishop knew, to make no further comment, to ask the scene to offer nothing more than the tone that the words describing it might propose. Certain things seen or remembered, or things painted, or things that bear associations, could not be simply dealt with, or simply could not be dealt with, or maybe even both; they could be merely listed as though they were the last things left in the world, the little that we get for free. The emotion was in the commas and the dashes, and in the spaces between the words, and in the reticence, in the silences, and in the sibilant at the end of the last word of poem, a word that seems to hang there, not to end, or not to end too easily:

> the munching cows,
> the iris, crisp and shivering, the water
> still standing from spring freshets,
> the yet-to-be-dismantled elms, the geese.

Bishop's "Poem" has interesting echoes with an early poem by Thom Gunn called "In Santa Maria del Popolo," the first poem in his third volume, *My Sad Captains* (1961), and one of his best-known poems. Gunn's poem was also about looking at a painting, in this case Caravaggio's painting of the conversion of St. Paul, which hangs in a corner in a side chapel on the left at the back of the church of Santa Maria del Popolo in Rome. Gunn, too, was interested in what lay in the painting and what lay outside the painting but was almost part of it.

In this case, it was shadow: "I see how shadow in the painting brims / With a real shadow."

The poem was not about the painting, but as in Bishop's "Poem," it was about the watcher; it was as much about what the eye does and how the self could be offered something—a glimpse of something else, a realization of something much less certain than the image in the painting—as it was about what was actually seen in the painting.

As in the Bishop poem, the gazer in the Gunn poem was alone. As poets, both were in full command as they described the work in front of them, Bishop amused or maybe intrigued by the small marks her grand-uncle the painter had made, Gunn awed by the mystery of St. Paul's conversion, the "wide gesture of the lifting arms," as painted by Caravaggio. Bishop attempted what was close to a customary conversational tone in her poem, with regular use of a five-beat line, working from an iambic pentameter base but varying it, relaxing it, breaking it, coming back to it. But not enough for anyone to notice it too much.

Gunn, on the other hand, used eight-line stanzas with a more or less regular and clear, if often subtle, iambic pentameter, with some variants. The rhyme is *ababcdcd*, the rhymes clear and masculine. It was in these years his customary mode. The voice was eloquent, impersonal, hushed. Gunn was interested in toughness, in violence, in what we might called advanced masculinity, and thus this scene in Rome, painted by someone who was later "strangled, as things went, / For money, by one such picked off the streets," held his attention. He was, he said, in an interview with the *Paris Review,* "in quest of the heroic in the modern world. . . . Well, by the time I got to 'My Sad Captains' I was growing up a bit."

Thus in his poem "In Santa Maria del Popolo," Gunn turned, "hardly enlightened" from the scene, not only because the shadows in the church and in the work itself did not offer him much light, but because the idea for him of Saul becoming Paul, of a bully becoming a saint, was not an easy transformation; it was not some-thing Gunn's imaginative system was much in sympathy with, yet he remained fascinated by the idea of the heroic, and of Paul's conversion as a renewal of the heroic rather than a defeat.

Like Bishop, he now had a problem in his poem. He had described the painting. Maybe that was enough, just to leave it like that, to leave the watcher mildly puzzled, untouched and in control, to leave the poem as one of those poems that describes a scene and has nothing more to say. In turning, however, he allowed the watcher a sudden recognition of something, just as Bishop recognized the scene in Nova Scotia as belonging to her as well as to the painter, which forced the voice in her poem to find a new tone more helpless and suggestive and wisely open-ended than her usual tone. In the last stanza of "In Santa Maria del Popolo," Gunn turned and saw people praying in the church:

> Mostly old women: each head closeted
> In tiny fists holds comfort as it can.

Suddenly, he was writing about the powerless, the weak, the supplicant. "I suppose," he told the *Paris Review*, "I acknowledge other kinds of life in . . . 'In Santa Maria del Popolo,' in that I'm speaking about the old women as well as the heroic gesture." The eye, which had been contemplating power and grandeur, now became tender. Gunn varied his meter in the next line as he watched. As he moved from the heroic to the defenseless, he moved from the iambic to the spondaic, managing to gather up emphasis on the two words he wished to utter, which were new words for him. He had been somehow shocked into pity by turning from the shadows and the mysterious image on the road to Damascus toward the powerless world, much as Bishop had come closer than she ever had before, or would again, to making clear what the landscape of childhood and its loss mean to her. Gunn wrote: "'Their poor arms are too tired for more than this."

We wait, then, for the final word that must rhyme with "this." The terms had been set for the ending of the poem. Thomas Wyatt rhymed the word "this" with "kiss" in "They flee from me that sometime did me seek"; Shakespeare in Sonnet 35 rhymed the word "this" with "amiss," and in Sonnet 72 rhymed it with "is"; Ben Jonson rhymed "this" with both "is" and "kiss"; Yeats in "The Cold Heaven" rhymed, or half-rhymed, "this" with "ice"; each of these rhymes offered a sense of clanging certainty and finality. Now, however, Gunn was aware, as Bishop had been in her poem too, that his ending must be tentative, strange, and open; it could not be a single conclusive word.

In the meantime, he needed a rhyme for "can" in the fourth to last line, and this could easily be found as "man" in the second to last line. So the end of the poem could read thus:

> Their poor arms are too tired for more than this
> —For the large gesture of solitary man

And now Gunn needed his final line, where he wanted the rhyme with "this" to have a weak sound to emphasize that the poem was ending, as Bishop's had ended, with a kind of sigh rather than a ring of certainty. He wrote:

> Resisting, by embracing, nothingness.

I read, or I would like to read, "nothingness" here partly as a simple word, the abstract noun from "nothing" almost restored to the language of poetry by Gunn from its tedious time in the language of philosophy, where it had languished and become a cliché. (Gunn made his early admiration for Sartre clear in interviews.) Nothingness. Its dying fall, the emphasis on the first syllable and the last two dying away in a sibilant, made its sound close—obviously, its sense also sets it apart—to Bishop's comma and last two words in her last line of "Poem": "the yet-to-be-dismantled elms" and then a comma (which silently contained an emphatic "and"), and then the final two words, "the geese," and this suggested that the observers, so powerful and in control at the beginning of both poems, have been oddly weakened by something only half-understood. They have been rendered themselves powerless as the mastery of the material moved by a sudden twist into the mystery of the material; the meter reflected the mystery in the weakness of its final footfalls.

It doesn't matter much whether Bishop ever read Gunn's "In Santa Maria del Popolo," and I do not wish to propose that she was "influenced" by it. It is more likely that she and Gunn, working with almost the same material, found a way in their tone and diction and the music of their meter of managing similar material—the solitary self, the watching of a picture, a gap, and then a strange, inconclusive, and almost exquisite realization—that had similarities. In both poems they almost enacted strategies of self-protection, which both of them as poets and as people had uncertainly and uneasily developed, being broken down briefly by something that they had looked at closely and almost had understood. And then they realized something more important than what they had almost understood. And then that, too, in a way we might describe as pure poetry, seemed finally to elude them as well.

Art Isn't Worth That Much

Thom Gunn once noted that Elizabeth Bishop had told him Robert Lowell was her best friend; Gunn seemed pleased to record that when he met Lowell a few years later and mentioned Bishop, Lowell said, "Oh, she's my best friend." What was peculiar or perhaps what was sustaining to the friendship was how little Lowell and Bishop ever actually saw each other. Bishop lived in Brazil from 1952, and when she returned to the East Coast of the United States, where she lived between 1970 and her death in 1979, Lowell was mainly in England until his death in 1977. They sent each other poems, and Lowell helped Bishop win prizes and deal with publishers. They wrote letters to each other. Mostly, between 1947, when they first met in New York, and Lowell's death, they seemed, as Lowell wrote, "attached to each other by some stiff piece of wire, so that each time one moves, the other moves in another direction." On the other hand, he also wrote to her in 1963: "I think I must write entirely for you." She became his most avid reader. In 1964 she wrote to him: "I'm afraid you're the only poet I find very interesting, to tell the truth."

It is notable that despite the closeness of their friendship, there were things that could not be easily mentioned. When Lowell wrote to her in 1950, for example, to say that his father had died, there is no evidence that Bishop made any reference to the death in return. Her long letter to him after his mother's death, in 1954, began: "What a joy to hear from you! Heavens—I've felt much better ever since; I hadn't realized just how worried I had been, I guess. I had heard vaguely . . . about the death of your mother and felt I should have written about that but scarcely knew what to say and of course do not even now." She made no other reference to the death of his mother in a letter filled with news and trivia.

Some of their exchanges remain fascinating, such as the letter in 1957 when Bishop read a draft of a poem (which later became "For Elizabeth Bishop 2: Castine, Maine") Lowell had written about her in which he mentioned that her mother had tried to kill her. "I don't remember any direct threats," Bishop wrote, "except the usual maternal ones. Her danger for me was just implied in the things I overheard the grownups say before and after her disappearance. Poor thing, I don't want to have it any worse than it was." The following year, it must have struck

Bishop with considerable force when she learned that Lowell, who had had a breakdown, was incarcerated in the same mental hospital where her mother had been. "My mother stayed there once for a long time," she wrote to him. "I even have some snapshots of her in very chic clothes of around 1917, taking a walk by a pond there."

Bishop was careful when Lowell published his volume *Life Studies*, which contained autobiographical or confessional poems, in 1958. When he asked her to write a blurb for it, she produced an elaborate note of support, writing of the personal section of the book: "In these poems, heart-breaking, shocking, grotesque and gentle, the unhesitant attack, the imagery and construction are as brilliant as ever, but the mood is nostalgic and the meter is refined." She concluded: "Somehow or other, by fair means or foul, and in the middle of our worst century so far, we have produced a magnificent poet." She liked the idea, she wrote to Lowell, that the confessional poems "are all about yourself and yet do not sound conceited." In 1960, when she read some deeply personal poems by Anne Sexton (which were often compared to Lowell's), she wrote to Lowell: "There is all the difference in the world, I'm afraid, between her kind of simplicity and that of *Life Studies*, her kind of egocentricity that is simply that, and yours that has been—what would be the reverse of *sublimated*, I wonder—anyway, made intensely *interesting*, and painfully applicable to every reader."

The following year she wrote to Lowell to complain about W. D. Snodgrass's personal poems, calling Snodgrass "one of your better imitators" and saying: "You *tell* things—but never wind up with your own darling gestures, the way he does.... I went straight through *Life Studies* again and there is not a trace of it, and that is really 'masculine' writing—courageous and honest." In 1974, complaining about a tendency toward the confessional and the explicitly personal in other contemporary poetry, she wrote to Lowell: "There's all the difference in the world between *Life Studies* and those who now out-sex Anne Sexton." In 1974 Lowell wrote to Bishop: "By the way is a confessional poem one that one would usually hesitate to read before an audience? I have many (they are a perfectly good kind) but have none in my last lot, and you have none ever."

Robert Lowell wrote the poem "Water" about being on the coast of Maine in the summer of 1948 with Elizabeth Bishop; he put it at the beginning of his book *For the Union Dead*, which he published in 1964. He sent Bishop a draft of the poem in March 1962, adding that it was "more romantic and gray than the whole truth, for all has been sunny between us. Indeed it all started from thinking about your letter, how indispensable you are to me, and how ideally we've really kept things, better than life allows really." In her response, Bishop questioned the accuracy of Lowell's opening line, "It was a real Maine fishing town," and his line "where the fish were trapped." "I have two minor questions," she wrote, "but, as usual, they have to do with my George-Washington-handicap. I can't tell a lie even for art, apparently; it takes an awful effort or a sudden jolt to make me alter facts. Shouldn't it be a *lobster* town, and further on—where the *bait, fish for bait*, was trapped—(this is trivial, I know, and like Marianne [Moore], sometimes I think I'm telling the truth when I'm not.) . . . 'The sea drenched the rock' is so perfectly simple but so good."

Lowell replied: "Your suggestions on 'Water' might be great improvements." The poem finally read:

It was a Maine lobster town—
each morning boatloads of hands

pushed off for granite
quarries on the islands,

and left dozens of bleak
white frame houses stuck
like oyster shells
on a hill of rock,

and below us, the sea lapped
the raw little match-stick
mazes of a weir
where the fish for bait were trapped.

Six years later, Bishop sent Lowell a postcard from the Art Institute of Chicago of Winslow Homer's *Marblehead*, which is an image of two people in conversation on a coastal rock. "Out of all the masterpieces in this place," she wrote, "I chose this to send you, for obvious reasons."

Five years before he wrote the poem, Lowell sent Bishop a long and somewhat manic letter about that time in Maine. At the end of a day's swimming, he remembered,

you said rather humorously yet it was truly meant, "When you write my epitaph, you must say I was the loneliest person who ever lived." Probably you forget. . . . But at the time . . . I guess (I don't want to overdramatize) our relations seemed to have reached a new place. I assumed that would be just a matter of time before I proposed and I half believed that you would accept . . . and when I was to have joined you at Key West I was determined to ask you. . . . The possible alternatives that life allows us are very few, often there must be none. . . . But asking you is *the* might have been for me, the one towering change, the other life that might have been had.

Bishop, in her response, did not comment on this.

In 1974, when they had known each other for almost thirty years, Lowell wrote to her: "I see us still when we first met, both at Randall [Jarrell]'s and then for a couple of years later. I see you as rather tall, long brown-haired, shy. . . . I was brown haired and thirty I guess and I don't know what." Bishop replied, once more seeking accuracy from him and a sharper sense of detail: "Never, never was I 'tall'—as you wrote remembering me. I was always 5 ft 4 and ¼ inches—now shrunk to 5 ft 4 inches—The only time I've ever felt tall was in Brazil. And I never had 'long brown hair' either!—It started turning gray when I was 23 or 24—and probably was already somewhat grizzled when I first met you. . . . What I remember about that meeting is your dishevelment, your lovely curly hair. . . . You were also rather dirty, which I rather liked, too. . . . Well, I think I'll have to write *my* memoirs, just to get things straight."

In his letter remembering their first meetings, Lowell returned to the image of water. "But the fact is we were swimming in our young age, with the water coming down on us, and we were gulping." They were unusual as poets, or indeed as citizens, in that they did not have to work, as Lowell pointed out to Bishop in 1953; they both had trust funds that kept them going. They were both also only children.

The last poem in Lowell's *Life Studies,* "Skunk Hour," was dedicated to Bishop and written during a period when Lowell had discarded a number of poems about her. As he worked on it, he wrote to Bishop to say that it was "indebted a little to your Armadillo," but later he stated publicly that he "was intent on copying" the form of Bishop's poem "The Armadillo": "Both poems have an ambling structure, little stanzas and the final natural but charged image that gives the poem its conclusion and title." As David Kalstone pointed out, however, the poem was not simply an homage to Bishop and her work, but a way of using her tone and then moving away from it, a way of separating himself from her as much as moving close.

In Bishop's work, much was implied by what seemed to be mere description. Description was a desperate way of avoiding self-description; looking at the world was a way of looking out from the self. The self in Bishop's poems was too fragile to be violated by much mentioning. Slowly, the self then emerged with the same stark force that silence has in music. Bishop managed to unsettle the tone of a poem by watching a scene with a fierce precision, as though the scene or she herself would soon disappear; many of her best poems offered little real sense of the personal, nor any single meaning. The fact that the world was there was both enough and far too little for Bishop. Its history—or her own history—was beside the point. In an effort to praise Lowell, she mentioned a composer and a painter, Anton Webern and Paul Klee, whom she admired, who had used silence, blankness, minimal means; she wrote of their "modesty, care, *space*, a sort of helplessness but determination at the same time." Her poem "The Armadillo" opened:

This is the time of year
when almost every night
the frail, illegal fire balloons appear.
Climbing the mountain height,

rising toward a saint
still honored in these parts,
the paper chambers flush and fill with light
that comes and goes, like hearts.

What Lowell saw her do was find something
moving, an armadillo, and offer it in the poem
a resonant and disruptive mystery, a task and
function that were surprising, not fully clear,
and then all the more powerful for that. In the
poem Bishop may have implied a great deal
about her own helplessness, but she managed
also to suggest that such an implication might be
both taken for granted and also fully taken in by
the reader and felt. For Lowell, such an implication was precisely and openly and only what he
wished the poem to have. He wanted, in his own
words in another context, to make the scream
clang. He saw what could be done in the tone of
Bishop's poem by using short lines, with three
beats, against a longer line with five beats. He
adapted this system of short and long and short
to superb effect for the last stanza of his poem:

I stand on top
of our back steps and breathe the rich air—
a mother skunk with her column of kittens
    swills the garbage pail.
She jabs her wedge-head in a cup
of sour cream, drops her ostrich tail,
and will not scare.

In "Skunk Hour," Lowell had found a set of metaphors that were loose, suggestive, and ambiguous enough to encapsulate the personal plight he had outlined more clearly, perhaps even more flatly, in some of the earlier pages of *Life Studies*, but sharp enough to push further, or dramatize his place in the world more fully, than any of his merely confessional poems. It would, as David Kalstone wrote, launch "him into his true subject, investigation of the debilitated historical and personal forces that had shaped his life." His dramatization of this subject would culminate in a number of magisterial poems, such as "Waking Early Sunday Morning," "The Fourth of July in Maine," and "Near the Ocean" in his volume *Near the Ocean* (1967).

To some of the other poems in *Life Studies*, the ones where Lowell mentioned members of his grand family by name, as though they were personages, such as "My Last Afternoon with Uncle Devereux Winslow," Bishop's response should be read ambiguously. "I must confess," she wrote, "that I am green with envy of your kind of assurance. I feel that I could write in as much detail about my Uncle Artie, say—but what would be the significance? Nothing at all. He became a drunkard, fought with his wife, and spent most of his time fishing . . . and was ignorant as sin. . . . Whereas all you have to do is put down the names! And the fact that it seems significant, illustrative, American, etc., gives you, I think, the confidence you display about tackling any idea or theme, *seriously,* in both writing and conversation."

Not having the confidence gave Bishop her power. The idea of "nothing at all" fascinated her all her life. Writing to tell Lowell how wonderful it was when he named his posh ancestors was one way of dealing with him. (Bishop's grandfather's firm had built the Museum of Fine Arts in Boston and the Boston Public Library.) It is useful to remember that it was only in the poems she was not allowed tell a lie; the letters are different. Even the ones that attempt to be honest and true should be read as forms of relaxation from the grim business of telling the truth in poetry.

Both Lowell and Bishop drank, and both wrote poems about drinking and hangovers. In February 1960 she wrote to him: "Please send me the poem called 'The Drinker'—I have a sort of sonnet called 'The Drunkard' but I have never been able to decide whether it's any good or not." In April she wrote again: "Oh, I think your drunkenness poem is going to be superb! It started me off on mine again—mine is more personal and yet a bit more abstract, I think." In July 1960 she wrote to say that that she did not think she had commented on his poem "The Drinker," which he must have sent her: "I find [the poem] even more horrendous in PR [*Partisan Review*]. . . . The most awful line for me is 'even corroded metal' . . . and the cops at the end are beautiful of course—with a sense of release that only the poem, or another fifth of Bourbon, could produce." (Lowell would have understood that "horrendous" and "awful" here, coming from Bishop, were terms of praise.)

The poem "The Drinker" ended with this image:

> Out on the street
> two cops on horseback clop through the
> April rain

to check the parking meter violations—
their oilskins yellow as forsythia.

Bishop liked the poem enough to feel free to correct its detail. "As a cook," she added, "I feel I should tell you that soured milk is NOT junket, but the picture is all too true." (Lowell replied: "The junket was a joke, I know milk turns to clabber.")

Then, having corrected him, she began to compete with him—it is hard not to feel that their correspondence was kept animated by a well-bred but rather fierce and oddly loving lifelong competition: "I have a poem that has a galvanized bucket in it, too—it is one I started in Key West—and I think I even used the phrase 'dead metal,' oh dear—but it has nothing to do with my 'Drunkard' one." While she had an earlier poem about a drunk called "The Prodigal" (which had lines that echoed lines of Lowell's "Mr. Edwards and the Spider"), the poem she was referring to remained unfinished, but she seems to have worked on it into the 1970s. It is a poem, or rather the bad draft of a poem, about her mother, dramatizing a scene from childhood and ending with:

But since that night, that day, that reprimand
I have suffered from abnormal thirst—

I swear it's true—and by the age
of twenty or twenty-one I had begun
to drink, & drink—I can't get enough
and, as you must have noticed,
I'm half-drunk now . . .

And all I'm telling you may be a lie . . .

In some of her letters to Lowell, Bishop praised
his work in general and some poems in particular but managed also to make clear her uneasi-
ness about some of his work, or her dislike of
what he was doing, while making sure not to
break their friendship. This occurred not only
at the time of *Life Studies* but when she saw the
poems that were to be included in his volume
of loose translations or versions of poems, *Imitations* (1961), which was dedicated to her. She
was smart enough, however, when she received
the manuscript, to send a telegram immediately:
"TRANSLATIONS ABSOLUTELY STUNNING. PROUD
AND PLEASED."

While Lowell had asked her to "let me know
things you question," it is possible he did not
really mean it. In any case, she waited for two
months to write him a detailed letter. "Once
again," as David Kalstone wrote in his book

Becoming a Poet, "her tone toward him is mixed, even confused—sometimes solicitous, sometimes disagreeing, then embarrassed by the sharpness of her disagreements."

Her letter began by saying how much she and Lota had enjoyed his translation of *Phaedra.* "It seems amazingly natural . . . but *pure*—but undated. Isn't real tragedy a relief for a change? I feel I've said all this to you before, of course. Anyway, seems a *tour de force* to me, and I hope something is done with it." The letter went on for some length before Bishop came to her view on *Imitations,* mentioning first that the dedication "made me shed tears." She was worried, she wrote, about how the poems would be received. "Your star is so very high now . . . and to publish things open to misunderstanding might produce a lot of foolish jealous haggling and criticism that you could easily avoid." Slowly, she began to correct what looked to her like mistakes in Lowell's French rather than freedoms he had taken with the translations. She mentioned that she had done translations of some of the same poems herself. She noted that in the last line of Rimbaud's "At the Green Cabaret," for example, Lowell had mistaken the words "un rayon de soleil arriéré" to mean a ray of sun "behind" rather than "a ray of late sun." Lowell accepted her correction. Also, she wrote, "tartines" meant "the little pieces of bread and butter given to French school-children," rather than Lowell's "raspberry tarts." He replaced "raspberry tarts" with the French word "tartines."

Unless Lowell was exceptionally thick-skinned, which he was not, her letter must have been difficult to read. On the other hand, since there is no joy greater than correcting someone else's French, it must have been a pure pleasure for Bishop to write. ("And now having damned everyone," she wrote to Lowell in 1959 after she had criticized Stanley Kunitz and Richard Wilbur, "I feel awfully cheered up.") "If you want me to," she went on, "I'd be glad to give you more benefits of my past experience in Rimbaud-translating. (But of course not if you don't want me to.) (I spent a month alone in Brittany once doing nothing much but that.) Sometimes it seems to me you sort of spoil his joke, or give his show away, by bringing up his horror too *soon* . . . . I just don't want you to lay yourself open to stupid or jealous misunderstandings."

The next morning Bishop got going again and wrote Lowell another letter. It was as though she had not written a letter the day before. "I've at last made up my mind," she began, "to attempt something very difficult. . . . I am very much worried by the French translations, particularly the Rimbaud ones. . . . The Rimbaud and Baudelaire poems are so well known that I don't think you should lay yourself open to charges of carelessness or ignorance or willful perversity." She then proceeded ("if you will forgive my sounding like the teacher of French 2A, I'll give you some examples") to repeat some of the earlier examples of errors in his French and add some new ones.

In his introduction to *Imitations*, Lowell pointed out that "the book is partly self-sufficient and separate from its sources" and that his "licenses had been many" but that he had "labored hard to get the tone." When Bishop was not questioning his understanding of French words, she questioned his very tone in these imitations. One poem struck her in the original "as so much more light-hearted than you've made it. . . . I just *can't* decide how 'free' one has a right to be with the poet's intentions . . . and of course it is for you to decide, anyway (thank heavens!)."

In her second letter, she suggested that Lowell should consult T. S. Eliot on the matter and added: "I feel I am running an awful risk and

I am suffering, writing this. I think you should consult someone both more scholarly and more 'in the world' than I am, while you have time to do something about it." Since Eliot was to publish the book in London, he also got involved in the argument, agreeing that *Imitations* was a good title and if Lowell used "the word translation in the subtitle it will attract all those meticulous little critics who delight in finding what seem to them mis-translations." While Eliot said that he enjoyed the book as a whole, he had his own quibbles. "You cannot use the term 'old boys' in England as an equivalent of '*vieux garçons.*' 'Old boy' in England means an alumnus of a public school and is not at all an equivalent so I suggest 'gay old dogs.'"

Lowell accepted Eliot's suggestion. He also changed "large heart" to "great heart" in the first line of his translation of Baudelaire's "La Servante," as Eliot had dryly pointed out that "the phrase 'large heart' suggests merely an anatomical misfortune."

There is no evidence that Lowell replied to Bishop's two letters until June 27—four months after they were sent, an unusual hiatus in their correspondence. It would be a mistake, however, to view this as pique. He was suffering, instead (or perhaps as well), from one of his break-downs. He wrote: "I'm O.K. and have been since April and have been meaning to write you since April, but I shy away from giving a lot of personal history. . . . I was in hospital for five weeks or so, less high and in an allegorical world than usual and not so broken down afterwards. Once more there was a girl . . . and once more a great grayness and debris left behind me at home." He then returned to the subject of his book *Imitations:* "My book is a lot bigger. . . . (I took all your suggestions). . . . The whole is much more worth dedicating to you now, and I hope you'll be pleased."

There is an undertow in the letters Bishop wrote about *Life Studies* and *Imitations*, a sense that she was containing herself, that the term "fair means or foul" which she used while praising *Life Studies* was not used idly, and that she was deeply uneasy about Lowell writing so openly about himself and his family as she was about the entire idea of the slackness of his translations. She did not say so, however, and not saying so was one of her most developed skills. But in 1972, when she saw drafts of the poems that were to appear in Lowell's *The Dolphin*, some of which were sonnets made directly from painful letters to Lowell from Elizabeth Hardwick, Lowell's wife of many years, after he had left her for the novelist Caroline Blackwood, Bishop finally could not contain herself.

In some of the sonnets by Lowell, Hardwick's letters were in quotation marks: "'I love you, Darling, there's a black black void, / as black as night without you,'" or "'I got the letter / this morning, the letter you wrote me Saturday. / I thought my heart would break a thousand times.'"

Bishop insisted at the beginning of a long letter that "I think it is wonderful poetry . . . they affect me immediately and profoundly." Then she continued by quoting from Thomas Hardy: "What should certainly be protested against, in cases where there is no authorization, is the mixing of fact and fiction in unknown proportions. Infinite mischief would lie in that."

She went on: "I'm sure my point is only too plain . . . Lizzie is not dead, etc.—but there is a 'mixture of fact & fiction' and you have *changed* her letters. That is 'infinite mischief' I think. . . . But *art just isn't worth that much*. . . . In general, I deplore the 'confessional'—however when you wrote *Life Studies* perhaps it was a necessary movement, and it helped make poetry more

real, fresh and immediate. But now—ye gods—
anything goes, and I am so sick of poems about
the students' mothers & fathers and sex-lives
and so on."

Later she sent Lowell a quote from Kierkeg-
aard, which seemed to sum up the difference
between her method and his as they came to the
ends of their lives: "The law of delicacy, according to which an author has a right to use what
he himself has experienced, is that he is never
to utter verity but is to keep verity for himself
& only let it be refracted in various ways." And
then she added, as though to take the harm out
of everything she had said: "But maybe that is
exactly what you *have* done?" But it is possible
that she did not really think so.

Lowell made alterations to the book as a result
of this letter, although he left in the sections from
the poems quoted above. Frank Bidart wrote in
his notes to the poems: "Lowell responded by
fundamentally changing the book. Several of the
poems in Hardwick's voice were muted by taking them out of direct quotation, placed in italics, their anguish and anger softened." Lowell
wrote to Bidart about Bishop's letter: "I've read
and long thought on Elizabeth's letter. It's a kind
of masterpiece of criticism, though her extreme

paranoia (for God's sake don't repeat this) about revelations give it a wildness. Most people will feel something of her doubts. . . . Now the book must still be painful to Lizzie, and won't satisfy Elizabeth. As Caroline [Blackwood] says, it can't be otherwise with the book's donnée."

As Lowell began to write many, many sonnets, which he published in *Notebook 1967–68* (1969) first and, then, revised and expanded, in three volumes—*History, For Lizzie and Harriet,* and *The Dolphin,* all published in 1972—Bishop wrote to him in 1971 to ask: "How are the sonnets going? Well—I think I have written *one*." If this question was not her epistolary style at its most mischievous, then she was more innocent than we know.

Among the sonnets Lowell produced, he wrote about her relationship to the North and South Atlantic:

you've never found another place to live,
bound by your giant memory to one known
       longitude.

In another, he rewrote his poem "Water" and made it a sonnet. When he had first sent her the draft of this poem in 1962, which had included lines about her ("One night you dreamed /

you were a mermaid clinging to a wharf-pile, /
and trying to pull / off the barnacles with your
hands"), Bishop wrote not only to correct details
but to remind him of something he had not included in the poem that she had recited to him
then, four lines of a verse (as she remembered it)
about Edna St. Vincent Millay:

> I want to be drowned in the deep sea water
> I want my body to bump the pier
> Neptune is calling his wayward daughter
> Edna, come over here.

It was her way of nudging him to be less ear-
nest. Now, he played another stroke in their game.
He renamed "Water" "For Elizabeth Bishop
(twenty-five years) 1. Water." In doing so he destroyed it, took all the calm, spare delicacy away
from the original poem, made the opening lines
sound as casually dead as so many of the lines in
these late sonnets of his (other lines, it should be
said, are startling and brilliant, but not these):

> At Stonington each morning boatloads of
>   hands
> cruise off for the granite quarry on the island,
> leaving dozens of bleak white frame houses
>   stuck

like oyster shells on the hill of rock.

Remember?

When he sent her some of the sonnets, she replied to say that she loved them. But she emphasized that she preferred the others to "Water." About this new sonnetted version of "Water," she wrote: "I am always dumbfounded by your capacity for re-doing things. . . . I think I'll try to turn that damned FISH [her poem 'The Fish' had become one of her most famous poems] into a sonnet."

Then she made a mistake; she wrote about how desperate she was. Lowell responded by turning this part of the letter, so unusually and painfully personal, into the sonnet "For Elizabeth Bishop 3. Letter with Poems for Letter with Poems." He wrote to her to apologize "for versing one of your letters into my poems on you in Notebook. . . . Too intimate maybe, and if so I humbly ask pardon." The poem—which often gave readers, myself included, their first glimpse into Bishop's personal life—began, as we have seen:

You are right to worry, only please DON'T,
though I'm pretty worried myself. I've
    somehow got
into the worst situation I've ever
had to cope with. I can't see the way out.

We would need perhaps Borges's Pierre Menard to tell us how long it took Lowell to make up these four lines. Perhaps as long as it took him to copy them out, or perhaps even quicker. Because Bishop's letter, written in February 1970, had included the lines more or less verbatim: "Well, you are right to worry, only please DON'T!—I am pretty worried myself. I have somehow got into the worst situation I have ever had to cope with and I can't see the way out." As David Kalstone has written: "Bishop's reply [to Lowell's poem], if she made one, is not among their letters. But his publishing this picture of her distress could not have pleased her."

It would not be fair, or even true, to say that Bishop waited and had her revenge. Things were never as simple as that between them, and it must always be remembered how much she loved him and admired him. For many years before the calmer tones of his final book, *Day by Day*, Lowell had worked on all his sonnets, or had them to "derange, or re-arrange," as Bishop put it; she had, as she said, just one sonnet (although she had written another one many years earlier, she had not published it). Her sonnet now was the last poem she finished, and its skinny perfection, compared to his garrulous hit and miss, must have given her pleasure, but it must have made her melancholy too that her "sad friend," as she called him, the only reader she really cared about, would not be there to witness the last word in their long conversation. (She outlived Lowell by two years.) She called her sonnet "Sonnet":

Caught—the bubble
in the spirit-level,
a creature divided;
and the compass needle
wobbling and wavering,
undecided.
Freed—the broken
thermometer's mercury
running away;
and the rainbow-bird
from the narrow bevel
of the empty mirror,
flying wherever
it feels like, gay!

The Bartók Bird

In August 1977 Bishop learned that Robert Lowell planned to visit her on North Haven, an island off the coast of Maine where she had rented a house. It was, she wrote, "a dream—peace and quiet and so beautiful." Lowell planned to come in the company of Mary McCarthy. Bishop had not forgiven McCarthy for *The Group*. (McCarthy, in a letter written to Bishop at the end of her life, which Bishop never received, denied that she had modeled a character in the book on Bishop.) In her correspondence, Bishop seemed to dislike McCarthy while remaining oddly fascinated by her antics. In 1967 she wrote witheringly to Lowell about her: "Sometimes I think that she could say a lot less and it would count for more."

She wrote now to both Lowell and McCarthy, asking them not to come to North Haven. "Day before yesterday," she wrote to Lowell, "and the day before that, seven, in all, guests left & although I love them all and we'd had a very nice time—it was just a bit too much." To McCarthy she wrote: "I'd be grateful if you *didn't* come over—at least not this summer. Maybe next, if I can manage to come back here."

At the end of her letter to Lowell, Bishop wrote: "Well, I'll see you in Cambridge or New York . . . and maybe in North Haven next summer if I can get back here again." Lowell, however, died at the age of sixty the following month in a New York taxi on his way from the airport. Bishop was still on the island when she heard about his death.

The following year she set about writing her elegy for him, the poem "North Haven," using her notebooks from previous visits where she had listed the names of birds and flowers. She used literary references as well, taking the phrase "in a dreamy sort of way," in the third line of the second stanza, from *Alice in Wonderland*, taking the phrases "daisies pied" and "paint the meadow with delight" from the end of *Love's Labour's Lost*. And there are echoes in the fourth stanza, when she names the birds, of Thomas Hardy's late poem "Proud Songsters":

> The thrushes sing as the sun is going,
> And the finches whistle in ones and pairs,
> And as it gets dark loud nightingales
> In bushes
> Pipe as they can when April wears,
> As if all time were theirs.

This poem, in turn, as Tom Paulin has noted, echoes a passage from Hardy's novel *Tess of the d'Urbervilles:*

> Another year's instalment of flowers, leaves, nightingales, thrushes, finches and such ephemeral creatures, took up their positions where only a year ago others had stood in their place, where there were nothing more than germs and inorganic particles.

Bishop had failed to write an elegy for her mother or for her lover Lota de Macedo Soares, despite her pale efforts, and the sense of this failure fills the tone of "North Haven," with echoes of Yeats's "In Memory of Major Robert Gregory," where there is no reference to Gregory until the sixth line of the sixth stanza, and Gregory is not named except in the title. Yeats's poem admits in the last lines that this death took all the poet's "heart for speech."

Once more, as her poem opens, Bishop is alone and watching. She is noticing; not thinking or remembering or analyzing. In the second stanza, there is that element of "coziness tinged with melancholy" to which Gunn objected, a sort of whimsical elegance. In the third stanza, the poem's gravity emerges softly, tentatively; in listing the flowers she is also delaying what has to be said and suggesting, with care and tact, that the world, so ready to drift, has to be noted and its elements listed as though they were ready to disappear.

There is no tonal shift in the first line of the fourth stanza: "The Goldfinches are back, or others like them," so that it is easy not to spot the grim suggestion that the goldfinches are in fact not back at all; they are dead. And thus Bishop has perhaps only prepared the reader's unconscious for what is coming, now that the white-throated sparrow's "five-note song," which might seem innocent, is, in fact, "pleading and pleading" and "brings tears to the eyes." (In a letter to Octavio Paz, Bishop calls the white throated sparrow "the Bartók bird.") And then she has to work out what word to use as an end-rhyme, a word that will rhyme with "eyes," since the third and fifth line of each five-line stanza of "North Haven" ends on a rhyme. In Sonnets 1, 2, 14, and 153, Shakespeare rhymed "eyes" with "lies," in Sonnet 29 he rhymed it with "cries," in Sonnet 60 with "arise," in Sonnet 83 with "devise," in Sonnets 141 and 149 with "despise." George Herbert rhymed it with "rise" and with "suffice" and also with "despise." It is one of those words in English that is ripe for rhyming. After all the years now, Bishop has everything open to her to make a statement, to "*Write* it!," as she herself said at the end of her poem "One Art."

In the next line, Bishop came as near as she could to stating something that was true; the "coziness tinged with melancholy" has gone, and it has been replaced by another sort of melancholy, a slow, stoical melancholy when she says: "Nature repeats herself, or almost does."

What the following line does now is oddly miraculous and is a slow, incantatory dramatization of the tentative and withholding nature of Bishop's process as a poet. It is clear to her for many reasons, some of them deeply personal but others arising from her view of the poet's predicament in her time, that there is very little that can be said, but there is much that can be suggested. In the meantime, words must be precise, emotion must not "too far exceed its cause." The last line of this stanza, whose final word must rhyme with "eyes," has six words, each in an iambic beat; there is a caesura after three, marked by a semicolon. The words are in italics, which suggest not emphasis so much as a voice whispering, a voice, as Lowell said, "talking in a full noisy room, talking until everything is quiet." The last three words each end with a sibilant and half-contain the word "sigh." And what the voice says now is:

repeat, repeat, repeat; revise, revise, revise.

The six beats here in the fourth stanza are part of a pattern. The first five lines of every stanza have five beats, and then the last line is longer, "a retarding hexameter," as Helen Vendler puts it, "a slow down at the close, as if unwilling to move forward."

It seemed odd and maybe fitting that a poet who had avoided writing elegies, who had kept the elegiac note between her lines and, instead, observed the world and made it seem more mysterious and made each aspect of it more singular with each poem, now managed in one of her last poems to write an elegy to an old friend without losing anything of her hard-won tone.

In the meantime, in San Francisco, Thom Gunn was fighting his own battle, working toward a looser style in his poems. "His poetry could accommodate a bit of relaxing," August Kleinzahler later wrote. In the first part of Gunn's 1982 volume *The Passages of Joy*, none of the poems rhymed or was written in a regular meter. Some of the poems in the book seemed almost occasional, like exercises; others seemed slack, although there was always a stray line, or a rhythm, or what Kleinzahler called "subdued music," or an observation, which made clear his enormous talent, a talent that now seemed restrained and in waiting. Gunn disliked the confessional style, which was fashionable as much as ever. In a poem called "Expression," for example, echoing Bishop in her letter to Lowell, he wrote some of his own worst lines to complain of others:

> For several weeks I have been reading
> the poetry of my juniors.
> Mother doesn't understand,
> and they hate Daddy, the noted alcoholic.
> They write with black irony
> of breakdowns, mental institution,
> and suicide attempt, of which the experience
> does not always seem first-hand.
> It is very poetic poetry.

Gunn did not publish a book of poems between 1982 and 1992. In 1991, the year before he published *The Man with Night Sweats*, his second-to-last volume of poetry, he wrote a piece in the *Times Literary Supplement* about the short poem in the sixteenth century in which he examined some poems by Sir Thomas Wyatt. There were sentences in his description of Wyatt's imagination that could equally be applied to Gunn himself, and to Bishop. Gunn wrote, for example: "The tentativeness and conditionality of the perception hardly diminishes its force: it is all the more powerful for being as it were unwilled and unforeseen." He looked in particular at a number of Wyatt poems that did not come to light until 1961; these were elegies for some of Wyatt's friends executed with Anne Boleyn by Henry VIII. "The range of [Wyatt's] feeling," Gunn wrote, "is considerable, for he thinks as he grieves." He wrote about "the understated force" of these elegies. In these poems, he wrote, "Autobiographical detail, however discreet and allusive, is given a sudden symbolic force, as in Yeats." But what Gunn does not mention in his essay was how plain and moving and direct these poems are, how unlike so much of Wyatt's work they are, so as to make the reader feel that they may not be by Wyatt at all, or maybe they are by Wyatt's wounded voice, fearful, grieving, suddenly clear, the "tentativeness and conditionality" all gone:

And thus farewell, each one in hearty wise.
The axe is home, your heads be in the street;
The trickling tears doth fall so from mine eyes,
I scarce may write, my paper is so wet.

When I asked Gunn in the early 1990s if he had read these poems before he wrote the elegies for his friends in *The Man with Night Sweats*, he agreed that he had but was, rightly, uneasy about any suggestion that he had therefore been influenced by them. It may be more accurate to say that both he and Wyatt experienced the death in quick succession of a number of close friends, and that Gunn, for one, had been skillfully avoiding writing directly from his own grief, or from his own dark emotions, because he was suspicious of poems that came too easily from such sources. And he had, in any case, other things to write about.

By the 1980s, as his friends began to die of AIDS in San Francisco, Gunn, in his late fifties, had created a body of work that notably dealt with the mystery of surfaces, the complexity of cities, the pleasures of wit, the pleasure of pleasure, the fun you can have with drugs, the peculiarity of people, and the poetics of precision and toughness, both physical and spiritual. He had also written love poems. He had still not written a poem about his mother's suicide.

In the seventeen poems that make up part 4 of his volume *The Man with Night Sweats*, Gunn, the least elegiac of poets, someone who described himself as "a cheerful and rather superficial person most of the time," produced the greatest elegies of his age. He used everything he knew, at times exploiting an impersonal, heavily metered and sharply rhymed style in which all the obvious or easy terms of feeling had been excluded and thus somehow the strongest and most authentic levels of honesty and accuracy in feeling had been managed by him and manipulated and set free. He stood close to grief and reason, like seconds to figures in a duel; he forced them to open fire on each other. At times the tone was, despite his "not having an aleatory bone in his body," as Kleinzahler put it, relaxed and conversational. In some poems, he succeeded in merging grief and reason, and in one, a poem called "The Reassurance," he produced a simple, perfect lyric:

> About ten days or so
> After we saw you dead
> You came back in a dream
> I'm all right now you said.

And it *was* you, although
You were fleshed out again:
You hugged us all round then,
And gave your welcoming beam.

How like you to be kind,
Seeking to reassure.
And, yes, how like my mind
To make itself secure.

It would be too easy to say that in Bishop's "North Haven" and these poems by Gunn, something had been released. Both writers were in possession of conscious wills as much as a dark and haunted unconscious, and their not writing about what must have mattered to them enormously must be taken seriously. Their refusal to write certain poems was not failure; it might be said that they had succeeded in *not* writing these poems. And it would also be too easy to say that these late elegies were in fact really elegies for the dead they had failed to write about. But there is a strange moment in one of Gunn's elegies, a poem called "Death's Door," in which he wrote about four friends who died in the same month and in which, actually, he mentioned his mother's death for the very first time. The poem begins:

Of course the dead outnumber us
—How their recruiting armies grow!
My mother archaic now as Minos,
She who died forty years ago.

Having written about his friends, their slow withdrawal from life, and their finding themselves "with all the dead," he returned to the image of "my mother" among the ancient dead. Just as Gunn himself, in his exemplary and exacting life as a poet, had managed perfect discipline and also managed to keep, most of the time, and for good reason maybe, memory barracked in, he imagined now his recently dead friends, the figures who peopled the elegies he finally wrote, and his mother, appearing in a poem more than forty years after her death:

They have been so superbly trained
Into the perfect discipline
Of an archaic host, and weaned
From memory briefly barracked in.

Efforts of Affection

What Bishop wrote is deeply personal; her poetry comes from a uniquely singular vision and set of imaginative systems. And yet what she wrote is also connected to the places where she lived; the personal was open to suggestion; her tone moved as she moved from Nova Scotia to Key West to Brazil and then to Boston. Also, her poetry and her development as a poet are associated with Robert Lowell and Marianne Moore, as though they too were places she visited, places she missed or avoided as she moved south and away from them, and north again when they had left, when the coast was clear. Both Lowell and Moore mattered to her; Bishop felt deep affection for both of them. However, it is also the case that she took what she could from them and then began to evade their influence, sometimes operating with great deliberation and care. She learned a great deal from them, but she was not prepared to live under their shadow.

Lowell rewrote her story "In the Village" as a poem; he made a sonnet from one of her letters. In neither case did he consult her beforehand. Marianne Moore, also without consulting her, and with the help of her mother, rewrote

"Roosters," to show her how it might be done. (The poet May Swenson also made a poem from one of Bishop's letters.) Not only by moving south, but by outlining in ways both gentle and severe her differences from him, did Bishop keep Lowell at a distance. But it was done over time. Bishop's urge to keep Marianne Moore at one remove seemed somehow more urgent, and was acted on earlier.

Moore and Lowell were the surrogate family she could rebel against. They could protect her, offer her advice, seek to influence her; they could also take advantage of her air of helplessness. But they could not hold her; she would always slip away.

Moore and Bishop met in the spring of 1934, when Bishop was twenty-three and Moore forty-six. It was the year before Moore's *Selected Poems*, with an introduction by T. S. Eliot, was published. In the early years of their friendship, Moore saw all of Bishop's new poems and prose pieces, and introduced her to the editors of the magazines in which her poems would appear. In an anthology called *Trial Balances*, which came out in the autumn of 1935, in which older poets introduced and commented on the work of younger ones, Moore chose Bishop and noted with pleasure the lack of emotion in Bishop's poems, their coolness: "One would rather disguise than travesty emotion," she wrote.

Slowly, however, as Moore began to suggest changes to poems, Bishop's stubbornness—or perhaps seriousness might be a better word—began to emerge, as well as the differences between the two sensibilities. Moore's poems were filled with surfaces and darting suggestions, phrase heaped upon phrase, striving for a supreme accuracy, noticing the world in the same way as a deeply eccentric microscope, or a weird, darting spy-plane, might; her poems were textured, like tufted fabric. If a portrait of a sensibility emerged from them, it was as though by accident, or from some energy released from the poems' strange rhythms. They were close to certain pieces by Stravinsky, all brass and disturbed tones, unashamed of their own noise, or indeed paintings by Kandinsky, unashamed of their own swirling colors, whereas Bishop's poems had the sad gaiety and inwardness and sparseness of Webern or Mondrian or Klee. Moore used syllabics gleefully, whereas Bishop stuck to the calm dialectic of the iambic beat. It was always clear that Marianne Moore's efforts to re-create Bishop in her own likeness would fail.

It is not as though the issues were always clear, however. There are times when some of the suggestions Moore made seem right, or almost right. Bishop opened her poem "Paris, 7 A.M." this way:

I make a trip to each clock in the apartment:
some hands point histrionically one way
and some point others, from the ignorant faces.

Moore rewrote these lines as follows:

I go from clock to clock,
From room to room:
Some hands point one way
Some another, from the ignorant faces.

Bishop wrote to defend the word "apartment" ("To me that word suggests so strongly the structure of the houses, later referred to, and suggests a 'cut-off' mode of existence so well— that I don't want to change it unless you feel it would make a great improvement.") But it is the removal of the weak word "histrionically" that matters more and might be right, and seems to suggest that Moore, in rewriting the opening of the poem, was suggesting a way in which Bishop already wanted to go.

Moore's notes and her own poems, despite their difference from Bishop's poems, suggested a way. In an essay written in 1948, Bishop began: "As far as I know, Miss Marianne Moore is The World's Greatest Living Observer." Bishop then made clear, however, that accurate description in itself is not enough; it must seem spontaneous, there must be a sense of the thing being described by an eye for which no detail is too small, but being described *there and then*, in the breath of the poem. She wrote too about the care Moore took in the use of metaphor. "Miss Moore does employ it carefully and it is one of the qualities that gives her poetry its steady aura of both reserve and having possibly more meanings, in reserve." She also wrote about Moore striking "in her verse . . . a tone of complete truth-telling that is compelling and rare." All these things—the art of using detailed and fiercely accurate description in a poem; the idea of holding something in reserve in a poem; and the notion of "truth-telling" in poetry—would become essential to Bishop's aesthetic but may in fact have always been there. They merely met their match in Moore.

Besides these ideas, Bishop took from Moore's actual poems and then learned to play them herself in a different key. The "waves as formal as the scales / on a fish" in the opening stanza of Moore's "The Steeple-Jack" has echoes in "He has scraped the scales, the principal beauty, / from unnumbered fish with that black old knife" in Bishop's "At the Fishhouses." (The word "fishhouse" appears later in "The Steeple-Jack.") So, too, in "The Steeple-Jack," the encroaching fog has echoes in the fog that is also vividly and minutely described in "The Moose," whose very title seems to offer a sly suggestive homage to Marianne Moore. ("S," after all, comes just after "r" in the alphabet.) Some of the images and words in Bishop's "Florida" take their bearings from images and words in Moore's "The Frigate Pelican." Bishop's image of the wasps' nest in "Santarém" echoes the wasp nest in Moore's "The Paper Nautilus." (The paper nautilus in question was actually given by Bishop as a gift to Moore.) The listing of wildflowers in "The Steeple-Jack" makes its way into Bishop's "North Haven," as the surprising beginning of the third line of the sixth stanza of "Elephants" ("As if, as if, it is all ifs") echoes the line beginning "*Repeat, repeat, repeat*" in "North Haven." Moore's poem "The Fish" ends with a single statement with six words of only one syllable: "The sea grows old in it." Bishop's poem of the same name ends with: "And I let the fish go."

There was in Moore's diction a sort of certainty, a sense of a personality driving the rhythm and the observation, and moving outward and then further outward in the tones and phrases of the poem, away from the self, if there ever was a self in these brittle and brilliant poems. So that when Moore wrote to Bishop in 1938 to say, "I do feel that tentativeness and interiorizing are your dangers as well as your strengths," it is obvious that something serious is being said, and that Moore is formulating something that will divide them as writers. These two things—tentativeness and interiorizing—will become Bishop's mainstays.

In the early 1940s both Moore and Bishop were under different sorts of pressure. Moore, who lived with her mother, was ill much of the time, as was her mother. Her protégée, Elizabeth Bishop, began a lifelong relationship with the *New Yorker* magazine in 1940; Moore had not at that time had a poem published in the magazine. Bishop, despite her success with the *New Yorker*, was still writing very little and had had her first book turned down by several publishers. She was drinking and suffering from asthma. But perhaps more important in the changing relationship between them was Bishop's poem "Roosters," her most ambitious and striking poem to date, which she sent to Moore. What happened next, as David Kalstone outlines in *Becoming a Poet,* was almost comic, and then it was not.

Moore and her mother stayed up late and rewrote the poem in full. They removed words they saw as crude and took out images of violence. They did not adhere to Bishop's three-stanza structure but included many stanzas of two lines and one of four lines. In a letter written in October 1941, Moore praised some of the individual lines and phrases of the poem and then explained why she and her mother had disliked terms such as "water-closet" and "the dropping-plastered henhouse floor": "Regarding the water-closet, Dylan Thomas, W. C. Williams, E. E. Cummings, and others, feel that they are avoiding a duty if they balk at anything like unprudishness, but I say to them, 'I don't care about all things equally. I have a major effect to produce, and the heroisms of abstinence are as great as the heroisms of courage, and so are the rewards.'"

Despite sticking to her guns, so to speak, on the words in "Roosters" in 1940, Bishop in 1958 would take the Moore-ish line about rude words in response to some poems by May Swenson and, as Kirstin Hotelling Zona has suggested, would almost take on the persona of Moore as she dealt with Swenson: "I don't like words like 'loins,' 'groins,' 'crotch,' 'flanks,' 'thighs,' etc. . . . Also the poems I like best, those I think almost everyone would agree *are* your best, almost never use them. . . . I am not saying this from any Puritanical feeling, I swear. They are in general ugly words that startle the reader in a directly physical way, perhaps more than you realize. We have come a long way in the last 100 years in freedom of speech and writing—but we are still not comfortable with these words, *usually.*"

She also wrote: "It's a problem of placement, choice of word, abruptness or accuracy of the image—and does it help or detract? If it sticks out of the poem so that all the reader is going to remember is 'That Miss Swenson is always talking about phalluses'—or is it phalli?—you have spoiled your effect, obviously, and given the Freudian-minded contemporary reader just a slight thrill of detection rather than an esthetic experience." In 1970, in a letter to Swenson, she wrote that she admired her poem "The James

Bond Movie" "all except the word 'boobs,' but I suppose I'm an old prude. No I'm NOT!—but I don't like certain slang words for things."

Bishop ignored the suggestions of Moore and her mother about "Roosters," replying to Moore that she wanted to keep in terms such as "water-closet" "to emphasize the essential baseness of militarism." (She also chose to keep the title, instead of "The Cock," which Moore and her mother had innocently suggested as an alternative.) "Roosters" was published as the lead poem in an issue of the *New Republic*, edited by Edmund Wilson.

There is another element in "Roosters," as Kalstone points out, that may have disturbed Moore as much as some words did, or the images of violence. This was what Kalstone calls "the unexplained private suggestiveness of many of Bishop's dawn poems." In other words, in some of Bishop's poems about waking in the morning there was a hint of another presence, a sense that she had not slept alone, and somehow there was also a hint, or maybe more than a hint, that the other presence was not a man. May Swenson has a poem about Bishop that teases out the coyness of some of her early poems. It is called "Her Early Work." It opens:

Talked to cats and dogs,
to trees, and to strangers.
To one loved, talked through
layers of masks.
To this day we can't know
who was addressed,
or ever undressed.

Although Bishop and Swenson exchanged two hundred and sixty letters, Bishop had her reasons for maintaining her distance, as an unfinished and unpublished poem by Swenson from 1961 or 1962 makes us understand:

I was nuts
about you. And I couldn't say
a word. And you never said *the*
word that would have loosened
all my doggy love and let me
jump you like a suddenly
unhobbled hound wild for love.

Little Elizabeth
who still keeps me
wild at the end of your chain—because
I can't reach you, have never
pawed you, slaver at the thought
of you still, because, because

I have never *known* you years
　　and years—and love
the unknown you.

The idea of Bishop as someone "unknown" preoccupied Swenson. Swenson wrote to her in 1954 that she liked her poem "The Shampoo" "very much . . . but I would have a deuce of a time saying why . . . that is, it feels like something has been left out—but this makes it better in a way . . . a mysteriousness, although the expression is perfectly straightforward." Two years later, when she received "Four Poems," she wrote again: "I don't understand the Four Poems, that is, I get their *mood*, but I can only imagine what they are talking about—my imagination goes pretty wild and comes back with strange answers. . . . Reading these four poems I have to furnish them with 'meanings' from my own experience because you've left yours out. . . . I'm left outside here, sniffing and listening, and no use pounding on the door."

Of all the fragments, drafts, and unpublished poems included in *Edgar Allan Poe & The Juke-Box*, there is perhaps only one poem that could with complete confidence be included in Bishop's canon of mature and finished poems. It is an untitled poem from the late 1960s:

Close close all night
the lovers keep.
They turn together
in their sleep,

close as two pages
in a book
that read each other
in the dark.

Each knows all
the other knows,
learned by heart
from head to toes.

Bishop's morning poems may take some of their power from a need to chart sexual happiness, or even a threat to, or the slow ending of, sexual happiness. As Swenson came close to pointing out to her, Bishop managed to suggest this without saying it. In evoking her mornings, she needed to leave a mystery. The poems may be, as Swenson accepts, all the better for it.

Bishop and Moore remained very careful toward each other in the three decades after the rewriting of "Roosters." They wrote warmly about each other's work, Moore in 1957 writing a particularly beautiful and perceptive review of Bishop's translation of *The Diary of "Helena Morley."*

In 1955 Bishop published her second volume of poems, *A Cold Spring*. The penultimate poem was entitled "Invitation to Miss Marianne Moore"; it was based on a poem Pablo Neruda had written for a friend of his. In a letter to Robert Lowell in 1948, when the poem was written, Bishop wrote: "My best friend in N.Y. thought my poem about her [Moore] was 'mean,' which I found rather upsetting because it wasn't meant to be & and it is too late to do anything about it now, I'm afraid." The poem was published in a tribute to Moore in the *Quarterly Review of Literature* along with Bishop's essay about her work, "The World's Greatest Observer." Moore claimed to love the poem: "Never could I deserve so lovely a thing. I shall always be trying to justify it."

There is something silly and breezy about the poem; Thom Gunn's view of its cozy tone has already been referred to here. But it also seems to emphasize, using a forced note of gaiety, Moore's eccentricity; it suggests indeed that, on her way from Brooklyn to Manhattan, she might be comfortable on a broomstick. Also, Neruda's poem "Alberto Rojas Jiménez viene volando" was written to a friend who had died, and it may not have been the most tactful model for a poem about a friend who would live for many more years. It was a poem of great incantatory beauty that ended:

> I hear your wings and your slow flight,
> and the water of the dead strikes me
> like blind wet doves:
> you come flying.
>
> You come flying, alone, solitary,
> alone among the dead, forever alone,
> you come flying without a shadow and
>   without a name,
> without sugar, without a mouth, without
>   rosebushes,
> you come flying.

Bishop ends hers:

> Come like a light in the white mackerel sky,
> come like a daytime comet
> with a long unnebulous train of words,
> from Brooklyn, over the Brooklyn Bridge, on
>   this fine morning,
> please come flying.

Just as Bishop's last poem, "Sonnet," seems to be a way of addressing Robert Lowell's unevenness by a sharp-eyed and chiseled perfection, making clear that the use of minimal effects could have oddly enduring and memorable results and thus establishing Bishop's difference from Lowell, this poem to Moore seems a poem of farewell, of distance-creation and of sweet and good-humored mockery as much as a poem of invitation or sheer admiration.

"Manhattan / is all awash with morals this fine morning," Bishop writes, "with heaven knows how many angels all riding / on the broad brim of your hat." It may be a fit place for Moore and her hat, this Manhattan "all awash with morals," but it was hardly where Bishop planned to live.

When the poem appeared in a collection, it was followed by "The Shampoo," the last poem in *A Cold Spring*. This is the poem that made Swenson feel that something had been left out. But enough had been included. "The Shampoo," despite its mystery, was clearly an intimate love poem. It was, as Bishop wrote to Swenson, about washing Lota's hair: "I am awfully pleased with what you say about the little *Shampoo* & you understand exactly what I meant and even a little bit more. . . . The Shampoo is very simple: Lota has straight long black hair,—I hadn't seen her for six years or so when I came here [to Brazil for the first time] and when we looked at each other she was horrified to see I had gone very grey, and I that she had two silver streaks on each side, quite wide. Once I got used to it I liked it—she looks exactly like a chickadee.... Shiny tin basins, all sizes, are very much a feature of Brazilian life.... And I am surrounded with rocks and lichens— they have the sinister coloration of rings around the moon, exactly, sometimes—and seem to be undertaking to spread to infinity, like the moon's, as well."

Two years later, she wrote to Swenson: "No one but you and one other friend have mentioned *The Shampoo*.... I sent it to a few friends and never heard a word and began to think there was something indecent about it I'd overlooked. Marianne among others.... I'm afraid she can never face the tender passion. Sometime I must show you her complete re-write of *Roosters*— with all the rhymes, privies, wives, beds, etc. left out.... It is amazing, and sad, too."

It was not that Moore did not know about Bishop's relationship with Lota in Brazil. In August 1958, for example, she wrote to Lota to thank her for a gift. The tone is open and affectionate. "You do not seem quite so far away,

Lota, since the magic package arrived. If *only* you were here—you and Elizabeth."

Despite the warmth of her tone here, it is hard not to imagine Moore casting a cold eye on some of Bishop's poems that she had once read innocently, realizing now that her young friend was perhaps writing coded lesbian love poems all this time. One wonders if she noticed that Bishop's early poem "Chemin de Fer" could be read as a poem about female masturbation. Or that other early poems, some of which she read in manuscript, such as "A Miracle for Breakfast" and "Four Poems," secretly let us know that while Bishop later became a great poet of the spirit, she began, or partly began, as a poet of the flesh.

Bishop did not write an elegy for Marianne Moore when Moore died in 1972. She was already working on a long essay about her, however, which she read sections from after Moore's death but did not publish. (It was published in 1983, four years after Bishop's own death.) Called "Efforts of Affection," it was, with "In the Village," Bishop's finest prose piece. It was filled with comic detail about her old friend and mentor, with moments of insight and pure affection. Bishop also made a sharp defense of Moore as a feminist and as a poet: "Lately I have seen several references critical of her poetry by feminist writers, one of whom described her as a 'poet who controlled panic by presenting it as whimsy.' Whimsy is sometimes there, of course, and so is humor (a gift these critics sadly seem to lack). Surely there is an element of mortal panic and fear underlying all works of art?"

In that sentence, Bishop seemed to describe the underlying element in her own work, as much as Moore's. But soon in the essay she was back in the world, a world of odd things and peculiar stories that she loved and which distracted her from much else. She wrote of Moore one day abruptly asking her, "'Do you like the *nude*, Elizabeth?' I said yes I did on the whole." Moore replied: "'Well, so do I, Elizabeth, but *in moderation*.'" In "Efforts of Affection," Bishop managed to commemorate her old friend, with the same attention to detail as she had done in "North Haven" for Robert Lowell. But there was also the sense that, as she wrote about them after their deaths, she was determined to swim away from both of them, as she had done when they were alive, and swim away from much else, until she would find a stretch of dry land—or dry land close to water—where she could find refuge on her own terms.

North Atlantic Light

I am in Wexford now, in the southeast of Ireland, in a house close to the sea in Ballyconnigar Upper, or Cush, as it is called by the locals. My parents knew this stretch of coast; my father, in his twenties, with some friends, once rented a small house close to the strand near here. My parents also came on bicycles from the town of Enniscorthy on summer Sundays. There are photographs of them before they were married taken on the hill at Ballyconnigar Lower, which was also known as Keatings'; and then there are many more photographs of us as children when the family came here to spend the summer each year. While we lived our ordinary lives in the town, it is here, this small stretch of coast, this literal small backwater, where I feel closest to something I know, or remember, or wish to see again, write about again.

At first when I came back here, and even later, very little seemed to have changed, the smells were the same, or were familiar, as were some of the lanes and fields and ditches, and the mild good manners of the people were also familiar, and the light over the sea in the morning, and the way a rainy day can clear up in the evening, and the marly sand of the cliffs, and the strand it-self, and the hesitant, insistent low waves and the small stones of different shapes and colors (no detail too small) at the edge of the shoreline that make a hollow rattling sound as they hit against one another when a wave comes in or else they are pushed toward the back of the strand by the tide and left there when the tides goes out.

Some things have changed, however, and some things here are not familiar. There has been coastal erosion, so that the hill where my parents were photographed and which used to have a lookout on top has completely gone, and Keatings' house too, which was a landmark, has gone, and my father's first cousin Dick Whelan's house, which was close to the cliff, has fallen onto the strand, or most of it has. When I walk down there I can see the old fireplace and the back wall. And there are some new houses, including two that seem big and imposing in this modest land-scape, as well as this house that I am in.

The house we rented each summer is lived in by different people now. A porch has been added, and a bathroom and a new roof. In the years before my father died, there could be seven or eight of us sleeping there, and then aunts and uncles coming to visit. I have a memory of my

Auntie Harriet going back to the town one summer evening on her scooter, a memory of listening to the sound of the scooter fading and fading more, and then faint in the distance, and then not there. Of the dozen or so people who came to that house, only three of us are alive. And I am the only one who comes to this place still, who walks the lane past the house down to the ruin of Dick Whelan's house and then further down the opening in the cliff to the strand.

The painter Tony O'Malley lived in Enniscorthy in the 1940s and came to Ballyconnigar to draw and paint. He did some drawings of the hill above Keatings', and of the strand. As far as I know, he was the only painter who thought this mild landscape worthy of attention. Many of the Irish painters of his generation went to the west of Ireland, where things were wilder. Or they went to France. Later, in the 1970s and 1980s, Tony O'Malley, with his wife, Jane, spent a part of each year in the Bahamas. His tones and textures became more exotic then; he created vivid and exciting shapes and bright colors. He told me once that these new colors would begin to creep into his work in Ireland in the time before he would set out to spend time in Caribbean light. Just by his thinking about the light, or by his knowing he would soon be there, the work he made would start to change.

His work moved north/south; he came from northern light and had his eye nourished by the luscious glare of elsewhere. And then he came home. Home. I am here now. In 1976, three years before she died, Elizabeth Bishop compared herself to the sandpiper of her poem of that title: "Yes, all my life I have lived and behaved very much like that sandpiper—just running along the edges of different countries and continents, 'looking for something.' I have always felt I couldn't *possibly* live very far inland, away from the ocean; and I *have* always lived near it, frequently in sight of it." This is something she shares with many people, and even those who do not share this must dream of it, at least sometimes. It is hard to move too far inland.

In the mornings in Ballyconnigar, the sea is always different. It can seem closer sometimes, ready to spill over, when the light is clear, and then distant and forbidding, alien, almost steely sharp, stately, withdrawn, when there are clouds and no wind. In the mornings when there is sun, the light on the sea can be all glare, or buttery on softer days, or austere when there are clouds in the western sky.

Some years ago a friend let me know there was a small painting by Tony O'Malley for sale in an auction in Dublin and I should go look at it. I recognized the scene as soon as I saw the painting. At the bottom of it is written "1952 Ballycunnigar," with O'Malley's customary signature from those years. (He must have written the name of the place as he heard it.) The painting is small, eight inches by ten. It is of a cliff, a strand, the sea, the sky. It is of a scene that is not there anymore. It is the soft marl of the cliff that was below Keatings' house gradually going down to be eaten away, washed away, to become nothing. It is painted from the south, facing north. It has the sand below the marl in two shades, one more golden because it is in sunlight, the other darker because it is in shadow. It has to be a summer's day, late in the day, because the slanted light is coming from the west. The clouds over the sea are shaping up for rain but are cut through by light; perhaps they will blow away. And then there is the sea itself, an easy blue as it often is, with a low wave in white and then another low wave behind it. No rocks; no people; no obvious drama, just the world doing its work. What is strange is that it could be nowhere else in the world because of the incline of the cliff, the softness of the sand and the sea, and the precise and peculiar curve of the land going north. It is Ballyconnigar Lower as you move toward Ballyconnigar Upper in the years before they added the huge stones to stop the erosion; in the years before the erosion itself changed this landscape, lowered the cliff and altered the incline, so that soon it will be remembered by no one, and no one will recognize the scene in this painting.

Tony O'Malley saw it in 1952, and I saw it some years later. Both of us looked at it; he must have studied it closely to get it as exact as he did. It must have mattered to him to make a painting from precise looking and rendering, or finding shapes and colors that would approximate what he saw, but capture it, envision it, re-create it. I never looked at it like that. It was part of what was normal, what was there. But I remember it. I believed perhaps that it would always be there. I must have taken it in on the same summer days, or days like them, days a few years after the painting was done. In any case, we both were there. "Our visions coincided," as Elizabeth Bishop wrote in "Poem," on seeing a painting of a childhood scene, and then she tempered that with "'visions' is / too serious a word—our looks, two looks: / art 'copying from life' and life itself, / life and the memory of it so compressed / they've turned into each other." This feeling that we know somewhere, or we knew it, and it is "live" and "touching in detail," is, as Bishop says, "the little that we get for free / the little of our earthly trust. Not much."

Not much perhaps, but enough to be going on with. Or perhaps not.

4-18-17

MESSAGE	
UNSUBSCRIBE HOW TO KILL E	*10/04/20
WEIGHT OF 0	*10/11/20
WHATS WRONG WITH MINDFULN	*10/18/20
100 DEADLY SKILLS THE SEA	*10/18/20
12 DAYS OF DASH AND LILY	*10/18/20
12 DOGS OF CHRISTMAS	*10/18/20

▦ ACKNOWLEDGMENTS

I am grateful to Hanne Winarsky who commissioned this book; to Alison MacKeen, Daniel Simon, and Anne Savarese for their work on the manuscript; and to Ellen Foos at Princeton University Press. I am also grateful to Mary Kay Wilmers and the *London Review of Books*, where some of this material has appeared; to Sandra Barry for her willingness to share her deep knowledge of Bishop's work and life, and also to her and to Alexander MacLeod for their hospitality in Nova Scotia; to my agent, Peter Straus; to James Pethica for lending me his house in Nova Scotia; and to Ed Mulhall and Greg Londe for reading the manuscript.

◼ BIBLIOGRAPHY

Works by Elizabeth Bishop

Brazil. With the editors of *Life* magazine. New York: Time, 1962.

The Complete Poems, 1927–1979. New York: Farrar, Straus and Giroux, 1983.

Conversations with Elizabeth Bishop. Ed. George Monteiro. Jackson: University Press of Mississippi, 1996.

Edgar Allan Poe & The Juke-Box: Uncollected Poems, Drafts, and Fragments. Ed. Alice Quinn. New York: Farrar, Straus and Giroux, 2006.

Elizabeth Bishop and The New Yorker: *The Complete Correspondence.* Ed. Joelle Biele. New York: Farrar, Straus and Giroux, 2011.

Exchanging Hats: Paintings. Ed. William Benton. New York: Farrar, Straus and Giroux, 1996.

One Art: Letters. Ed. Robert Giroux. New York: Farrar, Straus and Giroux, 1994.

Poems. New York: Farrar, Straus and Giroux, 2011.

Prose. Ed. Lloyd Schwartz. New York: Farrar, Straus and Giroux, 2011.

Words in Air: The Complete Correspondence between Elizabeth Bishop and Robert Lowell. Ed. Thomas Travisano with Saskia Hamilton. New York: Farrar, Straus and Giroux, 2008.

Secondary Sources

Boland, Eavan. *A Journey with Two Maps: Becoming a Woman Poet*. Manchester: Carcanet, 2011.

Brodsky, Joseph. *On Grief and Reason: Essays*. New York: Farrar, Straus and Giroux, 1995.

Donoghue, Denis. *Connoisseurs of Chaos: Ideas of Order in Modern American Poetry*. New York: Columbia University Press, 1984.

Elizabeth Bishop and Her Art. Ed. Lloyd Schwartz and Sybil Estess. Ann Arbor: University of Michigan Press, 1983.

Fountain, Gary, and Peter Brazeau. *Remembering Elizabeth Bishop: An Oral Biography*. Amherst: University of Massachusetts Press, 1994.

Goldensohn, Lorrie. *Elizabeth Bishop: The Biography of a Poetry*. New York: Columbia University Press, 1992.

Gunn, Thom. *Collected Poems*. London: Faber & Faber, 1993.

———. *Selected Poems*. Ed. August Kleinzahler. New York: Farrar, Straus and Giroux, 2009.

———. *Shelf Life: Essays, Memoirs, and an Interview*. London: Faber, 1994.

———. *Thom Gunn in Conversation with James Campbell*. London: BTL, 2000.

Heaney, Seamus. *Finders Keepers: Selected Prose, 1971–2001*. New York: Farrar, Straus and Giroux, 2003.

Kalstone, David. *Becoming a Poet: Elizabeth Bishop with Marianne Moore and Robert Lowell*. Ed. Robert Hemenway. London: Hogarth, 1989.

Lowell, Robert. *Collected Poems*. Ed. Frank Bidart and David Gewanter. New York: Farrar, Straus and Giroux, 2003.

———. *Collected Prose*. New York: Farrar, Straus and Giroux, 1987.

Millier, Brett C. *Elizabeth Bishop: Life and the Memory of It*. Berkeley: University of California Press, 1993.

Moore, Marianne. *Complete Poems*. New York: Penguin, 1994.

Neruda, Pablo. *The Poetry of Pablo Neruda*. Ed. Ilan Stavans. New York: Farrar, Straus and Giroux, 2005.

Stevenson, Anne. *Elizabeth Bishop*. New York: Twayne, 1966.

Swenson, May. *Dear Elizabeth: Five Poems & Three Letters to Elizabeth Bishop*. Logan: Utah State University Press, 2000.

Wyatt, Thomas. *The Complete Poems*. Ed. R. A. Rebholz. New York: Penguin, 1978.

Zona, Kirstin Hotelling. *Marianne Moore, Elizabeth Bishop, and May Swenson: The Feminist Poetics of Self-Restraint*. Ann Arbor: University of Michigan Press, 2002.

▣ PERMISSIONS ACKNOWLEDGMENTS

Grateful acknowledgment is made for permission to reprint the following previously published material:

Excerpts from "Sandpiper," "In the Waiting Room," "Crusoe in England," "The Moose," "The End of March," "Song for the Rainy Season," "Cirque d'Hiver," "At the Fishhouses," "Over 2,000 Illustrations and a Complete Concordance," "Roosters," "Love Lies Sleeping," "Rain Towards Morning," "Little Exercise," "The Fish," "Songs for a Colored Singer," "The Bight," "The Burglar of Babylon," "The Armadillo," "Santarém," "Jerónimo's House," "First Death in Nova Scotia," "One Art," "Poem," "Sonnet" (1979), "Paris, 7 A.M.," and "Invitation to Miss Marianne Moore," from THE COMPLETE POEMS: